THE MOST IMPORTANT BOOK YOU MAY EVER READ!

IDEAS #8: SUCCESS OR FAILURE—In this constantly changing world of ours, with its complex forces all about us, we sometimes cry out that we're driven by the force of circumstance and yet, the Truth of it is, that we only do those things we choose to do.

IDEA #23: EVERY WORD YOU SPEAK—You think of everybody you talk to, and regardless of how great or how small that effect may be, you will have to agree that everything that you say has an effect on the hearer. I want to expand on this premise for one moment and tell you that there is one person who hears everything you say, and that person is you!

IDEA #34: NO SLAP-DASH LIFE!—Whatever you are doing, do it zealously, thoroughly and lovingly even if you are polishing the silver. Polish your silver until it's fit for kings. Do your daily work, willingly, gratefully, and happily.

50
IDEAS
THAT CAN
CHANGE
YOUR LIFE!
DR. ROBERT ANTHONY

B

BERKLEY BOOKS, NEW YORK

Dedication

I joyously dedicate this book to the thousands of students who have studied the principles of successful living with me and who have used these principles in their daily lives to find health, happiness, abundance and inner peace.

This Berkley book contains the complete
text of the original edition.
It has been completely reset in a typeface
designed for easy reading and was printed
from new film.

50 IDEAS THAT CAN CHANGE YOUR LIFE!

A Berkley Book / published by arrangement with
Sunland Consulting Corporation

PRINTING HISTORY
Previously published by New Thought Publications, Inc.
Berkley edition / November 1987

ISBN: 0-425-10421-4

A BERKLEY BOOK ® TM 757,375
Berkley Books are published by The Berkley Publishing Group,
200 Madison Avenue, New York, New York 10016.
The name "BERKLEY" and the "B" logo
are trademarks belonging to Berkley Publishing Corporation.

PRINTED IN THE UNITED STATES OF AMERICA

10 9 8 7 6 5 4 3

Contents

Introduction

My purpose in writing this book is to help you live a more effective life by sharing with you the information and observations I have accumulated through personal experience and in dealing with thousands of persons each year.

For years you have been told that all you had to do to succeed and lead a happier and more effective life was to start thinking right. Those who have been telling you to discipline your mind are correct, but they have not gone far enough. We all know, even in our early years, that simply making up our minds to succeed and lead a more effective life seldom works. There is, to be sure, a feeling of excitement when we are told that all we have to do is to make a firm decision to change and we can achieve what we want. Unfortunately, the next day of the week most of us have forgotten our high resolves and are back to our old negative habits again. Our New Year's resolutions are often in shambles by the middle of January.

Being determined to succeed and lead a more effective and creative life is not enough, because it does not go to the heart of the problem, which is *faulty perception*. Once we see things correctly, once we interpret our environment in the light of reality or "what is," we can change ourselves.

I have come to know people in all walks of life and I can assure you that they have not been effective or ineffective, or met with success or failure, as a result of intelligence or the lack of it, or because they had, or had not, made up their minds to succeed. Those that failed did so because they were viewing their environment incorrectly. They looked at things the wrong way and then started believing things that were simply not true about themselves, their families, their occupation, and life in general. And because of this, they began to lose touch with reality.

Man is the only animal who talks to himself. All day long you are talking to yourself and feeding yourself information about your environment. You are exactly the same as a programmer feeding a computer, except you are both the programmer and the computer. Your five senses do the programming and if you look at things incorrectly, you will be out of touch with reality, seeing the world only as you *want* to see it. A successful, happy life depends upon accurate feedback from your environment to your mind.

We perceive a situation, then we program our mind with what we think is the reality of the situation. This determines our mental process and our behavior which in turn determines how we perceive the *next* situation. So, we *perceive, believe,* and *behave.*

I have drawn from many sources to help myself and others to perceive, believe, and behave. This book contains fifty ideas in the form of observations and anecdotes that are meant to give you, to the best of my ability, a picture in sharp focus, easy to see, of the situations you and I, and the millions like us encounter in our daily life. Hopefully, these ideas will encourage you to perceive, believe, and behave in new ways that will enable you to experience the best possible life!

—Dr. Robert Anthony

Idea Number 1

• • •

GOLD IN YOUR CELLAR

What would you say if somebody told you that down in the cellar of your house there was a box full of gold coins? You might say many things in surprise, but one thing you wouldn't do, and that would be to ignore it. You'd certainly go down and bring up that box of gold coins and put it to use; and yet, has it ever occurred to you that most of us live out our whole lives with a box of gold in the cellar of our minds that we never even bother to use. Deep down below the surface level of thought lies that wonderful part of our mind which we call the "subconscious." Everything drops down into the subconscious and nothing ever drops out of it. It is the storehouse of memory, the vast subterranean repository of knowledge. To be successful we need to make greater use of it. We tend to live like paupers sitting at a bare table in a fireless room, not knowing there's a pot of gold in the cellar.

Our subconscious can be made to serve the daily needs of our lives. It can be made to work for us

productively; it can make of you a much more efficient person by acting the part of a good secretary of
the mind, reminding you of certain things that need
to be done at certain times by hunting up information
that the conscious mind has mislaid. Like a computer, every fact and impression received into the
conscious mind is still down there below the surface
level of thought in your subconscious mind. How
then do you set about using and developing these
marvelous powers? How can we take possession of
this secret kingdom of the subconscious mind? Well,
it certainly can't be done in a hurry. The latent
forces of the mind must be trained by a slow, system-
atic process of suggestion and given direction through
the exercise of our will and imagination.

Decide what it is that you want your subconscious
mind to do for you, one thing at a time. If you want
a particular problem solved, spend five minutes or
so, night and morning quietly realizing that the whole
thing is being worked out for you on the subconscious level. Then quite suddenly—Pop! Up will
come the solution, and it will be the right one,
because the subconscious is open at its source to the
inflowing of the wisdom of Creative Intelligence. If
you want health, concentrate on health; never enter-
tain thoughts of weakness or disease. Make a daily
affirmation of the reality of health and well being. If
you want success, don't think in terms of failure. If
you want happiness, don't dwell on your miseries or
disappointments. That which is daily impressed upon
your conscious mind will sink down into your subconscious mind and eventually will become external-
ized as experience. That's why it is necessary to
think thoughts that are positive, regenerative and
constructive. Remember always that the subconscious

mind is open at its source to the wisdom of Creative Intelligence. Trust this wisdom and you will make fewer mistakes, and experience a greater amount of health, happiness and abundance in your life.

Idea Number 2

• • •

WHO IS HOLDING YOU BACK?

When you were younger did you have great dreams, great ambitions to write or to paint, to start a business, or to do some other creative work? Most of us did. In fact, if we are completely honest with ourselves, most of us still cherish these ambitions this very day, but we excuse ourselves on the basis of other commitments. I have my job to do. I would love to write a novel, but I have to do my work. I would love to paint, but I have a defect in one of my eyes or some other completely fatuous excuse we develop for not fulfilling our desires.

Think for a moment about Caesar. Did you know that Caesar wrote his commentaries in his tent at night while all the rest of the Roman army was asleep and then got up the next day and went to battle? Did you know that Handel wrote his best music *after* his doctors told him he was going to die; that Beethoven wrote music *after* he was totally deaf? Have you ever thought that three of the great epic poets of our world Homer, Milton, Dante, were all blind.

Think of Hannibal and Lord Nelson; great generals that they were, each had one eye. Francis Joseph Campbell, a blind man, became a distinguished mathematician and musician. Do you find yourself bound around in some way and feel, "Oh no, not with my limitations. I'll never be able to do what I want to do."

Think again about the author of Robinson Crusoe, Daniel DeFoe; he wrote that novel while he was in prison. John Bunyon wrote Pilgrims' Progress while he was in jail. Luther translated the Bible while he was in the castle of Wartburg. Dante worked for twenty years while he was under exile and under sentence of death, and Don Quixote was written by Cervantes while he was in the Madrid jail.

And then perhaps you say, "This is fine, but I have my job to do." Well, my friend, I have news for you. Have you ever looked at the thickness of the book *Gone With The Wind*? Margaret Mitchell wrote *Gone With The Wind* while she was working full time at a newspaper. Do you think of yourself as physically handicapped? Did you know that Lord Cavanaugh, who was a member of Parliament, had neither arms nor legs, yet managed to put himself into Parliament by his own endeavors.

Just think of Shakespeare, who learned little more than reading and writing at school, but by self-teaching, made himself the master among literary men.

Think again about the treasured ambitions locked up in your soul. Look again at the excuse which you have used to prevent yourself from fulfilling your dreams. See it for the false thing that it really is. Cast it aside and resolve to express your creative *desire* through your own creative *activity*. Remember, you are the only person who can hold you back.

Idea Number 3

• • •

BECAUSE I DESERVE TO BE

Many years ago the Viceroy of Naples, Duke of Assuna, made a visit to Barcelona in Spain. In the harbor at that time was a galley ship full of convicts at the oars and the Duke went aboard the galley and called for each prisoner and asked him what he was doing there, and why he found himself in a galley pulling on the oars as a convict slave and he listened to the tragic stories they told.

The first man said that he was there because a judge had accepted a bribe from his enemies and convicted him falsely. The next man the Duke talked to said that his enemies had paid witnesses to speak falsely against him and that was the reason he was there. The third chap said that he'd been betrayed by his very best friend who'd escaped justice leaving him entrapped, and then finally the Duke got the one man who said, "My Lord, I'm here because I deserve to be. I wanted money and I stole a purse and I deserve what I now suffer." The Duke was absolutely astonished at this and he turned to the captain of the slave ship and said, "Here are all these men who are innocent, who are here by unjust cause and here is this one wicked man in their midst. Let us release him for fear that he should infect the others." The man who had confessed his wrong was then set free and pardoned, while those who continued to excuse themselves went back to the oars and back to the galley.

This is a true story and it's an interesting one because it's exactly what happens in our lives. We make some error of judgment and then we go through life trying to excuse ourselves for it, rather than accepting that we simply made an error. We blame somebody else, we blame circumstances, instead of saying, "I have dominion over my life. I am the only one that has any power in the processes of my mind and what I have thought has brought me to where I am this very minute. I am responsible for my thoughts and by changing my thinking, I can change my life." The moment anyone of us reaches this moment of Truth, we are free from the galley slaving of this life, free to live the life that was ours all the time.

Look back over your own life. Recognize the growing processes. Learn to forgive yourself and to love yourself despite your mistakes. Accept them. Forgive them. Love yourself for them and you're pardoned from the galley of life and you're free to live as you always knew you should live, in happiness, peace and perfect health. It all starts with taking responsibility for your past, present and future.

Idea Number 4

• • •

THE BOOK OF LIFE

Is there perhaps another book close by to where you are sitting or standing at the moment? If there is, do me a favor and pick it up. It doesn't matter what sort of book it is, just pick it up and look at it. Now take a new look at it; try to see it from a different standpoint from your normal view. Let's suppose this book that you hold in your hand was washed up on the shore of some desert island where the natives were intelligent and culturally developed, but didn't have an alphabet.

What would happen? They would pick up the book and they would look at the beautifully produced paper; they would look at the lithography or letterpress, and see the complicated designs of all the letters and they would think that this was a very interesting art form and would doubtless appreciate it from that standpoint.

Would they understand the book? Would they get any real benefit from the book? I hardly think so. Surely the paper and the ink marks are but a tiny shadow of the real substance of the book. The book itself exists in a higher dimension. It exists in the dimension of IDEAS.

Isn't this the way it is with our lives? We look at the paper and the ink of our lives, the living, breathing, eating, working, sleeping—all the normal functions of our lives and we say: "This is life." Just as if we were to look at the paper and the ink of a book and say: "This is the book." But we all know that within our lives there is a meaning, just as there is a meaning within the book; surely the whole purpose of this life is not to be the paper and ink of the book, but to be the *meaning* of the book.

Our life has, first of all, to have *meaning*. Take another look today at the paper and ink of your life. Today you are going to get the children off to school, or you are going off to the office, and this is fine. Without the paper and the print, we couldn't communicate the ideas in the book, but *look beyond* the apparent *surface* meaning of these everyday items in your life and see the *real* content of those things. *Feel* the *real meaning* of the things that you are doing.

You are created and placed on this earth to fulfill a purpose. *Feel* that purpose this day, *reach* beyond the surface meaning of your life and get a single glimpse of the purpose in back of your life. With this single IDEA you will move towards an understanding of the whole book of life. One tiny glimpse of the purpose in your life will lead you inexorably on to the search for greater and deeper meaning; and that search is never meaningless; it always leads you to a deeper and deeper answer and it will bring you a greater and more meaningful life.

Idea Number 5

• • •

WHITE ELEPHANTS

What do you say when you see somebody making any number of foolish decisions, acting unwisely, making wrong moves, and gradually building up and building up for an emotional, physical or financial crash? When the final crash comes, are you one of those people who turns around and says, "Well, all I can say is 'he asked for it!' "? Well, I guess we all say it, and the strange thing is that we're all right, because we do ask for it, literally, don't we? All the troubles in our life have come because we have asked for them. It seems odd sometimes to realize that, but it's true.

Desire, deep inner desire, is a powerful force, much more powerful than most of us realize. We wish for things very, very deeply and the very intensity of our wishes draws those things to us. But if they are the *wrong* things that we've desired, they bring us misery and pain. They don't belong to us; we try to cling to them but they pass away from us.

I think, perhaps, it's dangerous to concentrate too

much on getting a certain specific thing or things out of life. Emmet Fox once said, "Be careful what you wish for because you're liable to get it!" I think he was right. The desires in your heart move in a mysterious way that none of us really understand, and they are made manifest in our lives. So we should be careful that we understand what it is we are wishing for. You know, what we wish for might turn out to be a white elephant!

The old Rajahs in India, when they wanted to break a man they would give him a white elephant. The problems of cleaning it, feeding it and parading it would make a poor man of him—so it is in our lives. Many of the things we desire turn out to be white elephants. I think that life withholds from us any number of our foolish desires because they would only turn out to be white elephants anyway.

Perhaps, rather than desiring *things*, we ought to start seeking more *wisdom*. It's a lot safer to seek wisdom, because having wisdom you find that you have the equipment to deal efficiently and humanly with other people and their problems. Having wisdom, you won't rush blindly into foolish decisions that lead inevitably to that crash that will give other people the chance to turn to you and say, "Well, I suppose he or she desired it anyway. They really asked for it."

Many people give up asking for things when they don't get exactly what they want immediately. They want what they ask for, but they don't ask for what they *need* and there is a vast difference isn't there between the things that we think we *want* and the things we *need*. Just imagine if as a growing child, your parents had given you everything you thought you wanted; that time you reached up for the bottle of disinfectant to drink it; or that time you reached out to the fire to grasp the pretty flame. You thought you wanted it, your parents realized you didn't need it and that it would be of no good to you; indeed, it might harm you, so it was withheld.

There is a difference between the things we want and our basic needs. If we will ask not for things, but for wisdom to understand what is right for us, then we shall have everything that we need and we shall learn those were the things we really wanted all the time.

Idea Number 6

• • •

INACTIVE ACTIVITY

Are you an active person? I suppose that depends on your definition of activity. Are you busy "running about" most of the time? Do you think that makes you an active person? I wonder if it does? I don't think activity always demands action. I think there are times when our actions are an excuse for not knowing what we really want to do. A lot of time and energy is often wasted in fussing over nonessentials. We can ill afford such an extravagant output of strength which achieves actually nothing. Sooner or later we have to decide on what is important and what is unimportant, because if we try to do everything at once, we shall end up by doing almost nothing productive. This human mind of ours is a very delicate and complex instrument. It is subject to strains and stress both from within and outside, and too much pressure can often result in a breakdown.

Mental fatigue can be just as exhausting as bodily weariness. There's only one way to keep on going, and that's by a constant return to the quiet place of communication with the Inner Self within us. To rest quietly with the Source of all life and vitality, and that surprisingly enough, is activity; that activity which transcends our mental or physical activities. There is a point of stillness at the hub of the whirling wheel of time, and it's to that center that we must learn to withdraw if we're not going to be broken on the spokes or flung off the edge. This quietness at the heart of activity is the only place where this Inner Self can get to us. So if we want this peace we must put ourselves consciously in a position to receive it. This is the secret of renewal of strength; mental, physical and spiritual. Having found this truth, you will experience the confidence of the mind that has found its true center.

Activity does not always mean running about. The activity of this Inner Self is often in absolute stillness. When you take your car battery to the gas station to be charged, it stands up on a shelf with only two wires attached to it, and it seems to be completely dead, nothing's going on, and yet deep within the cells of that battery more activity is going on than at any other time in its life. I think it was Sir Edward Arnold who wrote, "Ye suffer from yourselves, none else compels, none other holds you that you live and die, and whirl upon the wheel and hug and kiss its spokes of agony." It is true that you're not bound to a constant whirl of activity and often you're most active when you can become completely still and allow this Inner Self to be active within you.

Idea Number 7

• • •

MISTAKES

Are you frightened of making mistakes? Many people are, not only people, but sometimes governments. Some time ago I read that the government of Uganda had given up broadcasting weather forecasts. It seemed that the African native listeners heard the broadcasts and assumed that these were government edicts and that the weather would conform. When they discovered that the weather forecast was wrong, they blamed the government, and thereby began to disbelieve everything else that the radio station sent out, saying that the whole thing is a pack of lies, just like the weather.

The Uganda government had a simple way out. They simply stopped giving out broadcasts on the weather. But I question whether this was really the right or the best solution, don't you? What is the point of discontinuing activity just because we make a mistake? We wouldn't get anywhere, would we, if everything we attempted and failed at, we discontinued?

Supposing as a small child, the first time you toppled forward and fell down, you quit and said, "Well, that's a failure. It's not going to work." You wouldn't have led much of a life would you? Supposing that the first time that you'd ever made an error in a simple arithmetic problem, you'd quit completely. You'd never be able to change money or go shopping or do anything, would you?

It seems to me that making mistakes is an essential part of growing and, if we avoid doing something because of the fear of making a mistake, we deprive ourselves of all that is good in growth and in life. Now, of course, you could project this argument into absurdity. You could do so by saying that if we learn from our mistakes, then let's make more mistakes, because the more mistakes we make, the more we will learn. I'm not suggesting this extension of the argument; I'm merely saying that to use the possibility of making a mistake as an excuse for not having what you want is simply ignorance.

Whatever mistakes you have made in the past have been a vital part of your education and simply means that you should dust yourself off and begin again; not just quit and give up because you made a mistake and because it didn't work. Every mistake that you ever made in your whole life has led to your current state of understanding. Bless your mistakes, give thanks for them, dust yourself off and go on again. You will doubtless make more mistakes, but you will learn from every single one and no mistake is ever fatal unless you make it so.

Idea Number 8

• • •

SUCCESS OR FAILURE

Do you consider yourself a success or a failure? It seems to me that the majority of failures in this life of ours are nothing more or less than victims of their own mental attitudes. There isn't any philosophy of life by which a person can achieve things that he doesn't believe he can achieve. Yet the way always seems to open up for the person of determination, the person of faith and courage. It's the victorious mental attitude, the consciousness of power and the sense of inner mastership that does the great things in our world. If you don't have this mental attitude, why not begin today to cultivate it?

In this constantly changing world of ours, with its complex forces all about us, we sometimes cry out that we're driven by the force of circumstance and yet, the Truth of it is, that we only do those things which we choose to do. Even though we may not want to go a certain way, we allow ourselves to go that way because it seems to offer the least resistance. We follow that path which is easier to follow, even though we know it will probably bring future discomfort and difficulties. We're always at the crossroads of decision, in business dealings, in our family relationships, in our life, world and affairs. There's always a necessity to choose and how important it is that we make the right choice.

You see, once we realize that the power to overcome any problem lies within us, we stop looking to other people or to circumstances outside us for help. When we begin to call intelligently on our Self, the inner Self of us, we find that we begin to tune in to an Inner Resource of mental power. The secret of that power is understanding the resource of our own thinking processes, our own attitudes. When we begin to realize that the power to do anything, to be what we want to be, to obtain anything that we want to attain, is within ourselves, then and then only, do we begin to live the life of success which is ours! I believe that nothing great has ever been achieved except by people who dared to believe that there was, inside them, some Power greater, superior indeed, to any circumstance which faced them.

Now I'm sure that any person that's believed this has been ridiculed by friends and neighbors; they've probably thought him or her to be some kind of fool, just as many people do today. They think it's foolish and so they go on with their daily grind, living with sickness and lack until death comes along, almost as an anticlimax and a relief. Are you going to be one of those people, or are you going to listen to that Inner Power which is yours?

Begin to use the constructive power of your mind. Use your power of vision, because your thinking is the current that runs this motor of power. Connect your thinking powers to this Universal Subconscious and you become a superperson. Try it. You will find that you've discovered the key to the solution of every problem in your life. Put simply, it means this: You can do anything you think that you can do if you think hard enough that you can do it! Let me say that again: You can do anything you think you can do if you will think hard enough that you can do it. Victory in any circumstance, success, comes *first* in the *mind*. See yourself as achieving that desire and it shall be yours.

Idea Number 9

• • •

ROAD BUILDER OR WALL BUILDER?

Do you consider yourself a builder of walls or a builder of roads? Everyone of us throughout this life is building either walls or roads. How do you see yourself? I came across this short poem by Evelyn Hartwich who put this most simply and most beautifully when she said:

> "Great roads the Roman built that men
> might meet
> Yet walls also, to keep men apart, secure
> New centuries are gone and in defeat
> The walls are fallen, but the roads endure."

Do you build roads, mental roads, by which you can meet and share yourself with other people? Or, do you erect mental walls that separate you from others? It would seem to me that all the endeavor and all the material substance that goes into providing a wall of separation from other people is a complete waste of labor and materials because that wall can never, never stand.

The Truth is that we are Spiritual Beings, created

in Spiritual unity with all mankind and that our puny human walls of separation can never stand in perpetuity. But the roads, that's another story. That's different. Do you build roads that join you with other people, the mighty turnpike arteries of intellectual communication with people that come into your daily life in business; do you have this communication that transcends your business contact?

What about quiet avenues of shared emotion? Do you build roads from your heart to other people's hearts, the roads of common understanding, the roads of shared happiness, shared sadness, uplifted hearts joined together in common courage? Do you build these types of avenues, or the quiet lanes of love and understanding? These need no paving with words. They are leaf-covered lanes of a smile, a touch, or just a look that says, "I know, I understand, I love you." Do you build these types of lanes, for these are ever enduring. Nothing can destroy these.

Take time today to determine whether you are going to build walls with wasted manpower, wasted mental endeavor, wasted spiritual substance, in an attempt to separate yourself from your fellow man, or decide whether you are going to build intellectual arteries of common mental enjoyment, broad emotional avenues of shared experience and leafy lanes of unspoken spiritual unity. As you decide to build with your thinking processes, you will condition the nature of your world. It can be a world of walls, walling you in, or a world of roads that you can travel into joy eternal. The choice is up to you.

Idea Number 10

• • •

NOT IN OUR STARS

Do you think of yourself as being a lucky person; or an unlucky person? Do you think you get more than your share of the good breaks in life; or do you think you get more than your fair share of the bad breaks? When we're thinking about those hopes and dreams of ours that didn't come true, and those ambitions of ours that came to nothing, we're often apt to put the blame on that something called fate, or good and bad luck. And it really is nonsense, isn't it? Some of us say, "It's in the stars," or, "It wasn't in the stars." We talk to cover up our own shortcomings. We make our own luck, good or bad, by the nature of our consciousness. I think that Shakespeare sums that up very well in Julius Caesar when he says, "Men at some time are masters of their fate, the fault dear Brutus is not with the stars, but in ourselves." We underlings might indeed be masters of our own fate if only we could bring all our thoughts and actions into line with the creative purpose for our life. If only we could align our thinking with our purpose, then we indeed would become masters of our own fate. But how few of us are really prepared to trust our own Inner Guidance? Oh no, we prefer to rely on our judgments, and our past conditioning and when things go wrong, we're prepared to blame God or fate, or the stars, or something else that didn't go right.

If the past, all the past, could be played out before us, acted out in every detail, we should soon see when and where we went wrong, and we would be able to see in the play acting of our past, the very point at which we left the right road to follow a wrong star. We would see where we made the fatal mistake. We made the choice, you see. God gave us the gift of life, but He also gave us the gift of free will. We are the ones who make the choices that either make or mar the human life. Any time we want to, we can change the choices, and accept a different kind of life. Don't blame the stars for your problem, blame yourself because you acted like an underling, rather than one who is created in the image and likeness of the Great Reality. It is our faults and failings that throw grit in the wheels of destiny, and not some blind fate trying to trip us up, to hurt us or harm us. The Great Reality seeks only to pour into our lives the unformed substance of absolute good. Whatever we do with it by the nature of our consciousness is our responsibility. Out of every circumstance good can be made. We have within us the ingredients of good in every circum- stance, and as we accept this circumstance, you'll find the so-called fates are suddenly behind, and all goes well in our world. Why? Because we have aligned our path with the path of Creative Intelli- gence that always guides us to the perfect solution. All we need to do is to be open, responsive, and receptive to our own Inner Guidance.

Idea Number 11

• • •

THE GIFT PACKAGE

Do you like pretty packages? Most of us do. I had an interesting thought about pretty packages when I stopped in at one of the very beautiful department stores while I was traveling. I was looking at some merchandise and at the next counter there was a lady looking for a special kind of fancy soap. It was not the kind that one buys normally for one's own use, which comes three bars to a package and is a very ordinary soap, but each bar is wrapped in transparent paper and then is protected by a little cardboard box, and this box itself is wrapped in transparent paper to make it a tight and shiny fit. Then these little boxes sit in a cardboard tray and that too is wrapped in a colored transparent covering. Then there was a beautiful paper ribbon and a tiny bunch of imitation violets. Quite a package just for three humble cakes of soap intended to get you clean. Then I had the shock of my life when the lady serving at the counter smiled very sweetly and asked the woman customer a question that just threw me over. She asked, "Would you like me to gift wrap it for you?" I couldn't believe what I was hearing.

Isn't this just like so many things in our own lives? Here is the soap, perfectly normal, useful soap that becomes wrapped around so many times that we begin to lose sight of the original objective. The original objective in this package was to provide soap with which to clean ourselves. Yet by the time we had it wrapped and wrapped and overwrapped, the original soap becomes completely lost in the issue. We are far more worried about the packaging than getting clean.

In our lives all too often we are so concerned with the packaging, the gift wrapping over gift wrapping, tinsel over tinsel, that we lose sight of the basic material of life. I mean livingness its very self. All too often we become too concerned in job, home, family, finances, that we lose sight of the very livingness which we are. You see, underneath all the tinsel of day to day existence you are the living expression of Life itself. If that sounds like a platitude, it isn't. You *are* the living expression of Life itself. This means that you are the living expression of the power of Creative Intelligence. Don't allow the wrapping and the overwrapping of this life to allow you to lose sight of that all important concept because when you recognize yourself to be the living expression of Creative Intelligence, you begin to live life the way you were intended, and you have life gloriously beyond your wildest dreams.

Idea Number 12

• • •

RELEASE THE PAST

Do the names of Burke and Hare mean anything to you? They were once famous, or should I say, notorious characters. These two men discovered that there was a very good business to be had in digging up recently interred bodies and selling them to medical schools. This was back many years ago, around 1827. A terrible thing, of course, but ask yourself, are you perhaps a grave robber yourself? I don't mean to shock you, or to be disrespectful, but many of us are grave robbers without knowing it.

You see, every time you dig up an old grievance or an old mistake by rehearsing it over and over in your mind, or worse still, by talking to somebody else about it, you simply are ripping open a grave, and you know right well what to expect to find, don't you?

Live in the present, resolve your present problems, prepare intellectually for the future, but let the past ALONE. Just leave it. This is what the Great Teacher meant when He said, "Let the dead bury the dead.'' To think about the past and to live in the past is death. Every time you do so you strengthen to just that extent your belief in Time and in Time's limitations. You make yourself older, weaker and you bring on your own senility. God says, ''Now is the day of salvation, Behold I make all things new!'' —and God knows best.

Make it a rule for yourself that you are not going to mentally embrace any negative thing that has happened to you up to this very minute, and keep that rule. Life is much too precious to go grave robbing. The past is the past, it's gone; release it. This is the greatest secret of handling all our grievances, all our blunders, all our disappointments, all our failures—release them. You do this simply by writing them off in your mind; cleaning the slate of your mind and refusing to think of them as having any present existence. You see, the only existence that they can have is in your own mind.

The present is full of wonder and interest, and therefore, is such a glorious prospect for all of us that it is just plain foolish to waste our spirit and our substance on things that are dead. Leave the past. Release it. Set it free. Don't go robbing the grave, overturning bones of dead mistakes, failures and past events. This is a new day. Rejoice and be glad in it. Leave the past in the past.

You are made for this day. This is the HAPPIEST DAY, THE MOST SUCCESSFUL DAY, THE HEALTHIEST DAY OF YOUR LIFE. Know this for a Truth—if you release the past!

Idea Number 13

• • •

THE TOOLS OF THE MIND

Do you try to cut your lawn with a pair of scissors, or do you try to open tin cans with a pen knife? Of course you don't. You run your home with the most efficient tools you can find and afford.

But what about your life? What sort of tools do you use to run your life? You see, every thought we think, every word we speak, every deed we do and everything we allow ourselves to possess has its effect upon our physical body and its part in deciding the environment and the kind of people that we draw to us. If we sometimes get what we call punishment, or a raw deal, we, ourselves, created that thing, although perhaps unconsciously.

Within each one of us is a great mechanism for creation. You might call it the chamber of imagery and thoughts. In it are materials that we use to create. The tool that we use to shape our thoughts is our imaging power—imagination, we usually call it. This imaging power, like all other God-given faculties, is under our own control and our own direction.

It would seem sometimes, judging from the outer experiences of our affairs, that our image maker, our imagination, is also a bit of a mischief-maker, because it brings forth, in the body and affairs things that we don't care to claim for ourselves.

But the law is that the bringing forth in the body and affairs is always according to the picture and the pattern that we hold in the mental image. Sadness, sickness and poverty are indications that something is wrong with our mental machinery. We form a poverty consciousness or a sick consciousness by letting thoughts of poverty or sickness stay in our mind until the imaging power lays hold of them and crystalizes them in our life.

The best time to conquer any wrong thought, is the moment that it enters the mind. That's the moment where it is the weakest. But even better than conquering a thought when it enters the mind, is to try to prevent it from entering at all. A faithful doorkeeper of thoughts, a vigilant watchman over the imaging power will allow only thoughts of a constructive character to pass over the threshold into the chamber of imagery.

It is important to exercise conscious control over our thoughts. Every thought has a bearing on that which appears in our life and affairs. The one way to bring about a change in present conditions or situations is to make a definite change in thought habits. We have a great responsibility when it comes to thinking. We must remember at all times that our mental attitude, our thoughts and words, are the creative or destructive influences in the world in which we live. Do you constantly say, "I can't, I'm sick, I'm too poor, I'm too tired?" You deny yourself the power, health and prosperity which is rightfully yours. Thoughts of envy, malice, jealousy, anger, pride, hypocrisy, hate, cause your body to reflect disharmony and diseases.

Think and use the tools of imagery wisely and say, "I am well, I have plenty, I have limitless energy, I am at peace with my world and with all men," then you open the way for health, success and happiness. If you are loving and kind, if you treat all men and women honestly, charitably, you will soon find yourself in the kingdom of all good. Life will indeed be rich and rewarding.

Idea Number 14

• • •

THE WEIGHT OF THE "I"

Did you ever think about the weight of the letters of the alphabet? Did you ever consider the alphabet as having a weight? For example, what is the weight of a capital "I" with no dot over it in comparison to the small "i," the little one with the dot on top? Sometimes there is a fantastic difference in weight. I wonder if it has ever occurred to you that in all the European languages, the English language is the only one that has a capital "I" anywhere in the middle of a sentence when it refers to the first person singular, "I," and that is the capital "I" that we see and give so much weight to. Sometimes we give it so much weight that it impedes our own lives.

The weight of the "I" can oftentimes limit things in our own lives rather than accent them. You know what I mean. Someone in a restaurant sits down, gasping, "I'm exhausted. I've been shopping for the last two hours. Where on earth is that waitress?" Well, it so happens that she has been on her feet for more than just two hours. Wouldn't it be a surprise to her if the customer said, "Isn't it hard; how do you cope with running about this restaurant in this weather?" Have you ever noticed how anyone of us objects to the weight of somebody else's "I" being greater than the weight of ours?

Someone once told me that nothing made her more angry than when she would say to her husband, "Oh, I have an ache in my shoulder this morning," and he would answer, "Yes, my arm's real bad too." Nobody likes to think that when they've got an ache or pain, somebody else has got a bigger ache or pain than they have. The weight of the "I" becomes so terribly important.

I am sure that you remember the occasion when the Master Teacher decided to retire to a place apart for awhile, but the people thronged around Him just at the very same time when the weight of His "I" must have been wanting solitude and peace. The crowd swelled to about five thousand, stormed around and pressed to see Him. It was impossible to hear or even touch Him. Now, how exasperated He should have been. He should have said that He came up here so that He could get some peace and quiet. But he didn't say that, did He? He thought nothing about His own comfort and frustration. He said, "Make them sit down." He didn't say, "Now where am 'I' supposed to sit in the midst of all this crowd?" He said, "Make them sit down," and He set about His task of feeding them all.

The greatest mark of a great person is basic humility. I'm not talking about subservience. This is not what I mean. I mean to recognize the weight of the "I" as balanced with the weight of the "U" and not preponderant over it. As you go forward in your world, try and see how long you can go without putting forth a weighty "I" and you will find that you will make a lot more friends than you have ever made before because the weight of the capital "I" is exactly the same as the weight of the capital "U."

Idea Number 15

• • •

WORRY IS A KILLER

Are you inclined to be a little bit of a "worry-wart?" I love the story of the man who went to the psychiatrist because he was worrying himself sick and the psychiatrist, through the use of hypnosis, was able to remove the worries from the man's mind and he went away cured and very, very happy. The following day he came back into the psychiatrist's office in an absolute tizzy. He said, "Doctor, doctor, I'm dreadfully worried," and the doctor asked, "What on earth are you worried about?" He answered, "Doctor, I can't remember what it is I'm supposed to worry about."

I guess that's the way many of us are. This is a worry-crazed world that we live in. Many of our present ills are due to worries, the ones that we acknowledge, and also the ones that we hide even from ourselves. Worry lowers the tone of the mind and wears down our resistance to disease and despair. Worry is a killer. Make no mistake about it, worry is a real killer. Why then do we worry?

Perhaps you say that you can't help it. Worry has become a habit and you can't break up a long-standing habit in a few months. That's true. I'll accept that, but if you're going to break it up at all, you'll have to start somewhere, won't you? You'll have to begin sometime, so why not right here and now? Even if your worries cannot be overcome in two minutes, you've got to start sometime. Will there ever be a better time to begin than now? Try to make this one day a worryless day for you. If you're anxious over any particular point, try to realize that the thing will either happen or not happen. Those are the two alternatives. If you are anxious about an impending event, either it will happen or it won't happen. That's a pretty simple alternative and your worrying won't make any difference about it, will it? It will only make you less fit to cope with the situation should it turn out as you feel it will. By the time the thing happens, you'll have so worn down your resources by worry that you may not be able to cope with it; but if you can divorce the worry, even if the worst happens, you'll find that you've got strength and courage to deal with it.

Give up the idea that things cannot go right unless you worry about them. Give up worry the way a swimmer gives up his water wings when he realizes that he can swim without them. If you've ever had swimming lessons, you'll remember you flopped wildly about in the water at first. You made a lot of effort, but it didn't seem to get you anywhere, then, suddenly, you let yourself go. "I've got it!" you cried, "I can swim!" and that's how it will be when you develop the technique of letting yourself relax mentally. "I've got it," you'll say, "I can swim in the sea of life, I can swim without worry." All the time that you worry you're simply thrashing about in the waters of life and virtually drowning yourself. Whereas, if you would simply be still and try to live this as a worryless day, you'll be on your way to learning to swim peacefully in the seas of life and you'll find that it's a much better life as a result.

Idea Number 16

• • •

FLATTER OR COMPLIMENT?

Are you a flatterer? Most of us like to compliment our friends, but there's a fine line, isn't there, between the compliment and flattery. To see and to say sincere, complimentary things about other people is a gracious custom and makes life more livable for all of us. But as always, just as with money for example, along with the genuine and the good, comes the counterfeit and the bad, and the counterfeit of a sincere compliment is flattery.

There are many degrees of flattery and there are as many motives that prompt us to indulge in it. Sometimes it's nothing more than a simple bit of apple-polishing, just like the school student taking an apple to the teacher in the hopes that a few flattering words may take the place of a little hard work and earnest study. There are times when we seem to be in an atmosphere of flattery with everybody trying to outdo everybody else and no really sincere appreciation or complimenting going on. To flatter somebody in the hope that there will be patronage, favors, or preferment can prove to be the most arduous and unsatis-factory kind of work, more difficult than the work that we would have had to have done that this flattery is meant to replace. Because you see, people who are given to flattery are dissuading themselves from work and yet doing harder work in the very flattery. Indeed, flattery is pretty much like a drug; once you start to flatter somebody, you find yourself with a tiger by the tail. Ever-increasing doses of flattery produce an ever-diminishing effect, until the result is completely negative. The person who lives by flattery rather than by merit, lives a precarious existence at best and would do well to learn, while there is yet time, that the same amount of work dedicated to constructive and honest purposes, brings a much better and safer result.

But, I suppose flattery is most malicious when it's used with the deliberate intention of blinding some-body's judgment or to weaken somebody's resolu-tion, to try to get somebody to act in a manner less worthily and less intelligently than they otherwise would, or to cause them to give up some point of principle. It was, I think, with this in mind that the Psalmist wrote, "With flattering lips and with a double heart do they speak." Of this type of flattery, we can well suppose that we're getting absolutely nowhere in a constructive and useful use of our mind and our life. Flattery can never be trusted. There's no friendship in flattery and there is, between the self-motivated word of flattery and the completely unmotivated, sincere word of appreciation, a chasm wider than the Grand Canyon.

As you go forth in life look for the good. See that which is sincerely good and give compliment where compliment is due, but do not attempt to buy peace of mind, social acceptance or business preferment by flattery. It is a false coin and in time will become your master.

Idea Number 17

• • •

LISTEN TO THE S.O.S.

I'm sure you remember the tragic story of the "Titanic," but I wonder if you know the story of the "California," which is so closely related to the story of the Titanic?

You will remember that back in 1912, Great Britain sent her greatest steamship, the White Star liner Titanic, across the Atlantic Ocean. The Titanic was the largest ship that had ever been built up to that time and it was claimed that it was completely unsinkable, yet halfway across the Atlantic the ship hit a submerged iceberg and sank very rapidly. Of the 2,000 passengers aboard, 1,517 lives were lost. There was, of course, a tremendous outcry about this tragic loss of human lives and a great investigation was conducted and the causes were found to include excessive speed on the part of the boat, insufficient and inefficiently manned lifeboats, but above all, lack of information about icebergs, and as a result, the International Iceberg Patrol was formed and stringent safety rules were brought into being, and that investigation yielded another very strange piece of information that few of us know about.

At the time when the Titanic went down, *just thirty miles away,* was another ship, the California! Now this was before the days of very efficient radio communication and radio operators were few and far between and that night the one and only radio operator on the California had closed down his board at ten-thirty and had gone to bed. An hour later, the Titanic's operator was sending out frantic "S.O.S." pleas, but the wireless set on the California was closed and deaf to those pleas for help. The Titanic actually sank while another ship which could have reached her side in less than an hour went sailing on her way totally unaware of the tragedy, and this, to me, is the greatest tragedy of the Titanic. The fact that help was available and somebody could have helped, but wasn't aware that help was needed!

There's a great lesson in this for us, isn't there? As you sail on the sea of life, somebody's life is going to run up on some sort of an iceberg, somebody is going to be in great difficulty and in that difficulty, they are going to cry out. But the sad thing about human beings that cry out, is that they don't cry out "S.O.S." or "Help me, I'm in desperate need." They react in anger, in sulkiness, in sarcasm or in some way that they just pray is going to get them attention. Take time to listen for the "S.O.S." of the other human ships passing over the sea of life. Don't hear, "I hate you." Hear the desperate plea that says, "Please love me. I'm hurt, I'm lost and I'm lonely." Don't hear, "Mind your own business." Hear, "Help me, I'm lonely and I need love." Those messages, those calls for help are to be found in every "striking out" that you meet this day. Don't be a "California." Know that the "Titanics" are foundering all around you, but that you can hear the "S.O.S." and give the help that is needed. That's why you were put where you are today.

Idea Number 18

• • •

CASTLES IN THE MIND

Have you ever thought how many wonderful people build castles in the air and then live in mental horror? They have these wonderful castles of the mind; they have a castle of joy, a castle that they call personal happiness and within this they live a life of joy that never palls on them. Or, they have this castle of achievement, where, in their mind, they feel themselves accomplishing wonderful things, doing fine 'work without committing stupid blunders and seeing themselves as really achieving something worthwhile. Then they have this other castle of companionship where they see themselves as a charming person, rich in friends and supremely necessary to the people that they love best.

In these castles of the mind they see themselves living out the good life and they themselves, as their true beings, set free, one with life, with a chance of living as they really are. But then, when they come down from these mental castles into their daily life, they sit in desolation and say that it's quite impossible to build up real happiness out of the little things that surround them. Other people have the great gifts and the opportunities and the human love and the recognition; other people have the marble and the granite and the polished oak that enable them to build temples out of their lives; but me, I'm left with the lumber and the clay that builds a hovel of life.

Well, it just isn't true, is it? We're never forced back from the great things into the little things. We are continually being urged forward from the little things to the greatest things of all if we will only open our eyes and see that nothing is really lacking *except* the resolve to build; the resolve to accept those castles in the mind as feasible and practical and come from this wonderful world of the mind, and *resolve* to build these sort of castles in our daily life. If you will bring your castles of the mind to the point of *resolve,* you can have them in your daily life.

Idea Number 19

• • •

THE BEST IS YET TO BE

How old do you think we are? I mean we—all of mankind. Do you think that mankind is in its early stages? Do you think that perhaps mankind has reached middle age and from here on it's going to be decline and further decline? Or, do you believe that mankind is approaching the end, and that within a short time mankind will be no more upon the face of the earth, or out in the galaxies?

Personally, I think that the human race is only just now coming out of its earliest babyhood, the greatest lies ahead of us. Today, mankind is like a child of twelve or thirteen years of age in the Cosmic Universe.

Scientists estimate that man has been on the earth a million years; and that's conservative. He's been here much longer than that and civilizations have existed for tens of thousands of those years. Most of those civilizations, now forgotten, and their remnants are buried underneath the oceans, or under the desert, underneath mountains, or great mounds. Yet notwithstanding all this—early antecedents—the human race is only now in its earliest childhood.

The greatest days of mankind lie before us. All the really great achievements of the human race are still unborn. Music of the future will surpass even the greatest names today. Beethoven, Mozart and Bach will be surpassed, just as they, in their day, surpassed the beating of crude, native drums.

Literature will be produced that will make the works of Shakespeare, Milton and the other great lights of our civilization look like children's story telling.

In art, the art of ancient Greece, never equalled since, will be overtaken and surpassed by new waves of spiritual inspiration expressing through the art of mankind.

The greatest engineering feats of today: bridges and dams, airplanes, electronics and atomics will be like toys compared to the engineering that is yet to come in the future of mankind.

Above all, man's understanding of himself: man's understanding of his spiritual nature and of his spiritual world will grow by fantastic proportions. The religious geniuses of the past will be as pygmies compared with the spiritual leaders of the future.

Probably the greatest advance of man will be the tapping of the vast reservoirs of strength, courage and wisdom which he has never before touched.

So don't worry about the future of mankind. Turn your own eyes towards *your* future, for the best is yet to be.

Idea Number 20

• • •

REACTION OR RESPONSE?

Are you a responder or a reactor? Let me explain what I mean. I was sitting here writing this book, deeply immersed in thought, when the telephone bell rang and my instant human reaction was, "Oh drat, here I am trying to get this work done. Doesn't the outside world realize that I don't want to be disturbed when I am trying to think?" I picked up the telephone and I was rather, if not angry, certainly unresponsive. I was reacting to the telephone bell, rather than responding. But immediately I began to answer the call. I discovered that it was somebody very kind and gentle on the other end of the line, somebody who was very helpful. I thoroughly enjoyed the conversation. I was warmed on the inside by it and I went back to my writing in a higher state of consciousness than I left it.

Now, why did I react to the telephone bell in this manner? Yet the person on the other end of the line didn't react to my reaction. There was a response, a warm response, and that response produced from me

46

a response, not a reaction. Do you see the difference, and do you see the infectious nature of response and reaction in your life?

As you go into your day and you're met with trying circumstances—the telephone bell rings, the doorbell rings, and there is a salesman at the door, somebody comes into your office when you're busy, somebody comes across from next door to have coffee when you're trying to get the housework done—recognize one thing. *Nobody comes into your life today without a Purpose!* Everybody comes to bring you a blessing! If you react to that blessing, you stand to lose it. You are the only loser. Whereas, if you respond to each person that comes into your life with love and warmth, then you attract a similar response from them and you bring love and warmth into your own life, which was the blessing they came to bring in the first place.

Don't shut yourself off from the blessings which come into your life today. Respond to each person that crosses your path in the knowledge that they come to bring you a blessing. Respond in love to that blessing and you shall have blessings heaped upon blessings, and it will be a glad day for you rather than a hard day because of your simple understanding of reaction or response.

Idea Number 21

• • •

RISING ABOVE INJUSTICE

What do you do when you have been unfairly treated; when you've got the wrong end of a deal; you've been unjustly handled? What do you do? Do you try to maintain a friendly relationship with the people involved? Do you manage to forgive and forget? Do you manage to release all your resentment and bitterness, or do you say to yourself, "Well, I'd like to be friendly; I don't want to go on hating somebody because of an injustice and I don't want to allow this bitterness and resentment to give me an ulcer, but if I do forgive and forget, the only problem is that I won't get justice anyway"?

Is this the way you feel? Do you feel that the only way to solve the problem is to hang onto your bitterness and your resentment and your dislike in order to defend yourself against the original injustice? You know, it doesn't make sense, does it, when you think about it. That sort of revenge and retaliation complex hurts you more than it does the person who has done you the injustice and doesn't really solve anything.

If you think about justice for a moment, I think that you will realize that real justice is based on the Law of Love. The more we are able to keep ourselves in tune with this Law of Love, the more likely we are to have justice in our own lives. We surely know that the more we are able to cleanse our heart from bitterness and resentment, the more real we feel ourselves; the closer we feel to our identity with good. We know that the more we are able to send out love and forgiveness, the greater is the sense of freedom that we have and the greater the inner power that we feel.

You see, the problem is that in maintaining our resentment, in maintaining our hatred, in refusing to forgive, we stultify our own Inner Powers and we lose in terms of personal productivity, happiness and peace of mind, more than the supposed injustice is costing us. Now supposing you measure it in terms of money and you say, "Now here is an injustice that is going to cost me ten dollars, but by hating and resenting, I'm going to get an ulcer that is going to cost me a thousand dollars."

That just doesn't make good trading sense, does it? You will find that if you can rise above the injustice you will gain more in inner strength than the injustice will cost you. Think about this. If you can really rise above it, if you can really get the strength to say, "Well, it's water under the bridge, I'll forgive and forget," you will gain more growth, more power and more strength than the injustice will cost you and you will come out on the credit side of the ledger of life.

Idea Number 22

• • •

THE SHADOW

When I was a little boy, my friends and I used to play a game called "Shadow Jumping"—each one trying to jump on the other one's shadow. We were very much aware of our shadow in those days. How long is it since you had a look at your shadow?

You may become aware of it in a subconscious sort of way when you sit down to read; you find that the light is in a bad position and that the shadow of your head gets in the way of your paper. You either move your chair or you move the light in order to get your own shadow out of the way. Most of the time we are completely unaware of our shadow. Yet in our own lives, all too often we are aware of the shadowy parts of our own lives rather than of all the light that shines in and through our lives.

If you will look for a moment at your shadow right where you are now, you will observe that the only way that you can see your shadow is to turn your back to the light. Just have a good look at your shadow now and you will find that your back is presented towards the source of light that projects that shadow.

This is exactly the way it is in your life. You become aware of the shadowy parts of your life or those parts which you personally consider to be shadowy; these may be health problems, family problems, money problems. You become aware of them when you turn your back on the source of light in your life. That light of Creative Intelligence is moving in and through you, through your body, through your life and through your affairs all day, every day—a light that shines for you to guide you into perfect health, perfect happiness and perfect fulfillment. If you turn your back on that light, you will be aware only of the shadows in your life.

Think about it for a moment. Just cast your mind into those shadowy affairs in your life and ask yourself, ''Is it true that these are generated by my failure to look at the good in my life?'' It is so easy to be aware of the problems in life, but how much time and thought do we really give to the glory of our life and it is only in relation to the glory of our lives that the shadows are seen. You see, the shadow only exists in comparison with the light source. If light were coming from every direction, you would not see any shadows.

It is our failure to turn towards the light, to turn towards the good in our lives, to look at it, to give thanks for it, to glorify it, that enables us to waste time looking at the shadow and living in the shadows of life. *Turn towards the light in your life and the shadow will hold no fear for you.*

Idea Number 23

• • •

EVERY WORD YOU SPEAK

Are you an effective speaker? I don't mean can you get up on a platform and address a large group of people. I mean in your normal everyday communication, are you an effective speaker? Of course you are. Everything that you say effects everybody that hears it. What sort of an effect do you have as a speaker? If you are a humorous person, people probably laugh at what you say. If you are an angry person, then you probably induce a certain amount of fear and a certain amount of resentment. This is the effect that you have. If you are a loving and charitable person, you probably induce a warm glow in other people. If you are a complimentary person, you probably increase other people's own self-appreciation.

Every word that you speak produces its effect on the hearer. Now, I'm sure you can believe that, can't you? You think of everybody you talk to, and regardless of how great or how small that effect may be, you will have to agree that everything that you say has an effect on the hearer. I want to expand on this premise for one moment and tell you that there is one person who hears everything that you say; and that person is *you*! Every other person hears only a part of what you say, but you personally hear every single word that you say. Therefore, whatever the individual effect you have on other people is a cumulative effect that you have upon yourself. Think about this—the power of your words and their effect on molding your life is tremendous.

If you want to be a prosperous person, don't talk with a cheap mouth. If you do, all you do is make other people feel poverty stricken as well, and the cumulative effect is on you. If you feel sick, don't keep voicing your sickness to other people. Every person you talk to gets a tiny segment of that impact, but your body receives the whole impact of everything that you say. Other people are effected by what you say, we agree; and you can, if you want, by a kindly word timely spoken, uplift somebody's life. If this is true, then surely you can uplift your own life, since you are the recipient of the cumulative effect of every word that you speak. You, then, are molding your own life far more than you effect the life of any of your listeners. Whether it is your own children that you are speaking to, or trying to direct, or whether it is people in the office or people who come to your home, you have an effect on every one; but you receive the cumulative effect of every one of those impacts.

Can you see here a great truth? By yourself, by your very own words, the effects that you have on other people is produced in you in a cumulative form. Can you not see that as you do unto others, it shall be done unto you? You mold your own life, effect your own life by the nature of the words you speak, and remember, you do hear every word you speak.

Idea Number 24

• • •

THE DUEL OF LIFE

A century or more ago men settled most affairs of honor upon the dueling field, and there was a time in history in Germany when dueling scars on the side of a man's face contributed to a handsome visage. A man was considered handsome if his face was laced with the scars of dueling. Bismark, the great states-man of the nineteenth century, was an outstanding duelist—he would fight a duel over anything. But one day he became very angry over a supposed affront that he'd received from a scholar named Professor Virchow. Bismark was so angry that he challenged the Professor to a duel. Now the eminent scientist was somewhat taken back by this since scientists aren't normally duelists the way that sol-diers are. But, because Bismark had challenged Virchow, that left the professor with the choice of weapons. Then came the gray early dawn on the day of the duel, and up to the dueling field drove the two carriages with the duelers and their seconds—and the usual doctor. They climbed out of their coaches and met in the middle of the field of honor and Bismark said, "It was your choice of weapons, sir, what have you chosen?" Professor Virchow produced two beautiful juicy sausages and explained to Bismark that since he was a scientist, he'd chosen these sausages as his weapon. One was filled with lethal germs, and the other was perfectly good eating. He turned to Bismark and said, "Come, choose your weapon and we shall eat together." Bismark took one look at those two sausages, realized that one meant certain death, then angrily turned on his heel and walked off the field in red-faced defeat. I always chuckle when I think about that! The duel that was fought with sausages! Not by banging away at each other, but by simply offering the opportunity to choose between life and death.

During this day you will be called upon to fight a duel. You are going to fight that duel a thousand times today. You are going to have a multiplicity of choices during your day today—how to respond to what somebody says, how to respond to what somebody does, what to say, what to do, and you'll have those two sausages in front of you—the poisonous or the healthy. You can think the poisonous, negative thought that in its own tiny way will drag you down into ill-health, death, loneliness and poverty, or you can think the good thought which will lift you up and lead you on to eternal life, love and happiness.

Each time that you are faced with the choice of what to do and what to say this day, think of Professor Virchow—think of those two sausages. Choose the good, choose the thought that is on the upbeat, turn away from jealousy, anger, negation, doubt and fear and guilt. Think thoughts of joy, love, life and laughter. Speak words of joy, love, life and laughter and those things will fill your day and fill your life.

Idea Number 25

• • •

ISLAND OF PEACE

Do you ever wish that you could just run away from it all? Do you ever yearn for an island far off in some distant sea? Or a cabin hidden away on the top of some remote mountain where you could get away from all the pressures of your everyday life? I suppose we've all felt like this from time to time. It seems that we're always in the throes of conflicting impulses. We want, first of all, to be in the middle of activity and achievement, and then at other times, we want to retreat into quiet and solitude. Is this perhaps because we've lost a sense of balance? Have we become impervious to the river of life moving through us? Is it possible that our timing is off? You know, the ambition and the urge to accomplish drives our minds mercilessly until both our mind and our body demand rest and replenishment. Periodically, we must have respite of some type from our turbulent, rushing, hectic daily existence.

Have you ever watched an old grandfather clock? The pendulum must swing both ways, an even distance in each direction, if it's to perform its function satisfactorily, and this is the sort of balance we need in our own lives. We push ourselves too hard without adequate time for rest and restoring of the body and the mind. We simply must make time to recharge ourselves, mentally and spiritually, as well as physically. We need a state of equilibrium and this has to be cultivated by contact with the inner Self of us. Even a few minutes of being truly in touch with ourself, our real Self, will restore our strength and our courage and our peace. It's not necessary to buy an island in the Pacific or a mountain in Hawaii, in order to achieve balanced life. I imagine life could be just as hectic on your island or on your mountain if you didn't achieve some inner mental peace.

Once we get onto this treadmill of daily pressures, we think that we've got no time for quiet or meditation, but we simply have to take time if we want to be a well-adjusted, happy and successful person. We're not sufficient unto ourselves, you know. We're dependent and one—with a Higher Power than ourselves and with patience, we can learn to keep our minds open so that we can turn from the pressures of the day to an inner calm within us. It doesn't take a great deal of effort. We have to simply become still and turn quietly within us to a Center of Peace which is ours at the center of our being.

You can find the peace of your island, or the peace of your mountain within yourself this day. You can have all the rest you need right within you.

Idea Number 26

• • •

DON'T LET IT SPOIL

What do you do when you have taken food out of the deep freeze, thawed it out to eat and then suddenly you get an invitation to go out to dinner somewhere? When this happens, it's quite impossible to use the food by freezing it again so you just have to cook it and eat it. I think that this is something we ought to think about in our own lives.

Mark Twain set this problem forward very simply and very clearly in a little joke he used to tell. There was a fellow that came round to Mark Twain's house twice every day trying to sell fish and Mark Twain kept saying, "No, thank you, no thank you." But finally, he felt that the man's sheer persistence ought to be rewarded, so he told his wife, "I am going to buy a fish from that man," which he accordingly did. When the fish was prepared for lunch, it was found to be highly unsatisfactory and when the peddler came around, Mark Twain went out and hailed him and said, "Look here, that fish wasn't edible. It was too old," and the fish man turned calmly and said, "Well, it wasn't my fault, boss. I gave you two chances every day this week to buy that fish and, if you were foolish enough to wait until it was spoiled, don't blame me."

Think about this. You have before you today, one whole day that has been taken out of the deep freeze of eternity and thawed out for you to use today. You can't live this day tomorrow, you can't live it the day after tomorrow, you've got to live this day today.

When do you live your life? Are you waiting for some never-never time when you are going to be happy? Are you going to wait until the fish spoils before you try to eat it? Are you going to allow this day to thaw out and spoil, or are you going to say, "This is a precious gift of God, the banquet of today. I am going to prepare it and eat it today. I am going to live this day to the fullest. I am going to say, one should never reject a gift. One should accept it with an open heart and an open mind and with thanksgiving."

This day is the greatest gift that you have ever known throughout your whole life—this one day. Don't allow it to spoil. Don't go through it with a feeling of apathy, defeat and loneliness—stir up the enthusiasm within you. Accept this day as filled with potential for success, happiness, love and joy—all these things are in this day. Don't just allow them to go to waste; go out there into your world today and accept them and don't allow the day to spoil. You cannot live this day tomorrow and you will never have this day again.

Idea Number 27

• • •

YOU BECOME WHAT YOU THINK ABOUT

Have you ever tried your hand at building—building something? Well, I suppose that everyone of us is building every single day of our lives. We are all busily engaged in building our consciousness during every waking hour. We are building a structure of attitudes, actions and reactions. The building we do is invisible and silent, and consequently it is probably overlooked by most of us.

Nonetheless, it's probably the most fundamental and most far-reaching activity in our whole life, this building of our states of mind and our attitudes. Every single one of us is building our consciousness all the time, although we are not even aware of it. Hour by hour, minute by minute, we are building good, or so-called evil, failure or success, happiness or suffering into our lives by the thoughts we think, the ideas that we harbor in our minds, the beliefs that we accept, the scenes, the events and the conversations that we rehearse in that hidden studio of the mind.

The actors that get into that hidden studio of your mind are those that will play out the drama of life for you. The drama of life is rehearsed in the radio studio of your mind and what appears outwardly is simply the presentation of the drama that you have rehearsed day by day, all unknowingly, building the script into your consciousness.

This building, this consciousness, this fateful edifice, upon the construction of which you are *always* busily engaged, is nothing less than your Self—your true SELF, your personality, your identity on this earth, your very life story as a human being, the central core of YOU, is that which you are building.

Now, if you are wise, if you are intelligent, if you exercise more common sense, you will, in the light of what you now know, build positively, and constructively. You will begin to take concern for that which finds a home in your mind. You will be concerned about the thoughts and attitudes that become the actors, rehearsing the drama of your life.

Supposing you were going to put on a play. You wouldn't go and find the least capable people that you could find to act in it for you, would you? Of course you wouldn't. You would go and find the most capable actors that you could locate. Let this be so in the radio studio of your mind. Bring into your mind these actors that can do a *good* job—love, kindness, security, faith, courage and wisdom. Give these a home in the studio of your mind because what gets your attention, gets you. You become what you think about.

Idea Number 28

• • •

THE MAGIC OF PRAISE

What sort of people are you going to meet on the road of life? Will they be happy people who will add to the happiness of your life, or will they be weary, run-down rather miserable people who will tend to drag down your life into a gray monotone? Would you like to have everybody that carries into your life happy and lifting you up with joy? There's simple way to do it, you know. All it takes is a simple word of praise. I don't mean insincere praise. I mean real, sincere, deep-down praise, not flattery.

I love the story about Johnny Figaro. Johnny Figaro was a thirteen-year-old Italian boy in New York. He was a real problem for his teachers. He seemed to be always fighting, spoiling the games of the younger children. He was rude to the teachers and the more he was punished, the more defiant he became.

In the 6th grade, he met a quiet, demure young teacher. One day, Johnny was sent inside at the recess. He clumped noisily to his seat and slumped down. The young teacher looked at him quietly and then said very pleasantly, "Johnny, how nice you look today in that clean shirt." He squared his shoulders and sat up straight. At noon, a frayed black tie was clumsily fastened under the collar of the shirt he was so proud of. The teacher very quickly noticed it and praised him on it. Next day, his knotted shoe laces were replaced with new ones and his scuffed shoes were shined.

The young teacher turned to all those who were handling Johnny and said, "Just praise him, he'll react. Just praise him."

Johnny Figaro grew up to become president of a state university in the middle west. A boy who would probably have been doomed to the slums and poverty became a great academician because somebody took the trouble to praise him. Everything blossoms and flourishes under praise. Praise is like water on a rose.

Determine that you are going to be an instrument for good in your world by praising other people. Look at everybody you meet and look for the praise-worthy in them and praise it. Give a simple word of honest praise and you will change the identity of everybody that comes into your life. Give a word of praise because you'll be acting as the Spirit of Love in God's world when you do this.

My friend, you are brought into this world to serve as the instrument of God's love. The easiest way to do it is simply to look for the good and to praise it.

Idea Number 29

• • •

THE PROBLEM OF PLEASING EVERYBODY

Do you sometimes despair of ever being able to please other people? Does it seem to you that you spend your whole life trying to please and help other people only to be rebuffed and falsely judged? If you do, let me share with you one short sentence of Montaigne's. He says, "A man has need of tough ears to hear himself freely judged."

You know, no matter how careful and conscientious we may be, someone is always sure to misunderstand our actions and our attitudes. When somebody is liberal with his means and his money, someone will always suggest that he's profligate or overextravagant. On the other hand, if you're conscientiously careful with your money, somebody will almost certainly say that you're a miser. If somebody's views are more liberal than yours, then he will brand you as being stuffy and conservative. If his views are more conservative than yours, he will complain that you're too liberal and when somebody opposes our position, on the other hand, we probably say that he's prejudiced. In all honesty we have to admit to ourselves that we probably often find ourselves condemning somebody else for what we would condone in ourselves.

If a person doesn't do anything, people will find fault with what he hasn't done. If he does something, then people will find fault with what he has done. While some people will congratulate what we do some of the time, those very same people will disapprove of what we do at another time. So it seems to me that whenever we're attempting to please other people, we have to remember that no person ever lived who ever pleased all the people all the time. In fact, I doubt if anyone ever lived who pleased one person all the time, not even himself.

Are you always pleased with your activities? I question it. No matter what course you may pursue, someone will wonder why you didn't do something different. So about the best that we can possibly do is just conduct ourselves conscientiously, according to our best understanding, following our sincere convictions, and keeping our minds always honestly open to the possibility that perhaps we're wrong, and then hope that others will forgive us our mistakes. We have to be tolerant of other people if we're expecting tolerance on their part. Above all, we have to remember the words of dear old Montaigne that "a man does have to have tough ears to hear himself freely judged" by others. If you find yourself being judged by your fellowman, think of these simple words, "You cannot please all the people all the time" and, if you destroy yourself by dissimulation, by trying to be all things to all people, then you never get a chance to express what you really are.

Go ahead and be what you are, as conscientiously

as you know how and know beyond doubt that you're going to have some people criticize you. Bless them, release them and go on doing the best that you know how. If you live as your real self, there will always be criticism.

Idea Number 30

• • •

THE SPARK PLUG

How is your car running these days? Have you perhaps had occasion to change spark plugs lately? If you have, you'll know that it's a very simple job. You drive into the garage and the mechanic opens up the hood of the car, looks underneath, takes off one electric wire, puts in a wrench and takes out a spark plug, puts a new one in, puts the electric lead back on and within five minutes you can be on your way. It's a very simple thing to change spark plugs, isn't it? But supposing you walked into a garage and asked them to change a spark plug and the mechanic came out and immediately started to take off the right-front wheel. You would probably think that he was slightly insane, wouldn't you, and you would protest vigorously that you didn't want the wheels changed, all you wanted was a new spark plug.

Well, the other day I had a friend come to see me. He has a new sports car and he explained to me that to change the spark plugs on one side of the car, it was necessary to take off the right-front wheel! This is absolutely true. Can you imagine the reaction of the owner the first time he drives into a garage and asks for new spark plugs? Out comes somebody and takes off the right-front wheel. He'd probably protest vigorously, as I said. Yet, my friend assured me that it was but a two-minute job to take off the right-front wheel and once that was off, the spark plugs were very, very accessible and simple to remove.

Now there's a lesson in this for all of us. We look at things in our lives and we see activities going on, like the taking off of a front wheel, and we wonder how on earth our lives work in this way. We're looking for the solution to a problem and a solution begins to come in some form which is totally incomprehensible to us. We expect our good to come to us in one way. We expect the solution to come into our lives in one very obvious way, like lifting up the hood and taking out the spark plug, but the solution begins somewhere entirely different.

We may be looking for the solution of a family problem when the real need is a change in jobs. We may be looking for a change in health when in Truth, the real need is a change in our own activities and our own thinking. The whole point to the story of the spark plugs and the front wheel is this: that we should not attempt to judge the way in which our problems are solved, or the way in which good comes into our lives. The total universe is a vast and complex organization. We can never understand the ramifications of Creative Intelligence in our universe and, therefore, in our own lives. What we could do is say, ''Fine, I accept that Life totally supports me, and I accept that there is good in my life, and whichever direction it may come from, I'll accept it, know that it is good and wait for the final outcome of good.''

Here then, my friend, encapsulated, is a great and vital Truth: DON'T EXPECT YOUR PROBLEMS TO BE SOLVED IN THE WAY THAT YOU SELECT. There may be a better way if you will put your preconceived ideas aside and open yourself to the inspiration of Creative Intelligence. It may mean taking off the front wheel of your life to get at a defective spark plug but the results will be better than you can possibly imagine. Trust your inner guidance and allow the solution to come from any direction and your problems will be solved easily and effortlessly.

Idea Number 31

• • •

EXPRESSING YOUR TALENTS

Are you a successful person or do you think of yourself as a failure? I suppose that every one of us must decide for ourselves whether we are a success or a failure, regardless of what the outside world thinks of us.

Indeed, if you look back through history you will find that many of those men who were the biggest successes in terms of outer acclamation, were complete failures in terms of their own inner aspirations. For example: Alexander the Great conquered the then known world, but he was never able to conquer his own violent temper—he wanted to do so very much that he considered himself a failure.

Napoleon won the undying devotion of millions of his subjects, but the one person he really wanted to love him, refused. That was Josephine, his wife. Although Napoleon was passionately in love with Josephine, she never returned his affection.

Then think of Goethe, one of the greatest poets and writers in the world, and yet he really wanted to be an artist; he wasted many years in his early life studying art when he really had comparatively little talent in that department and considered himself a failure as a result. Imagine Goethe thinking of himself as a failure!

Whistler, the great artist, strangely enough wanted to be a poet, but fortunately he realized his lack of ability and turned to art instead. But in terms of his poetry he was, in his own eyes, a failure.

Think finally of Hans Christian Andersen. Those fairy tales won him a fantastic place in the world of children's literature, and yet, he could only appeal to children through his writing. In face to face contact, children found him ugly and repulsive and he thought of himself as a failure in his contacts with children.

Now, take another look at yourself, and ask yourself: am I a failure or am I a success? If you are honest with yourself, I think that you will discover you are successful in those areas where you express those God-given talents that are yours and yours alone and that you are a failure, or you consider yourself to be a failure, in areas where you are trying to inflict your will upon a given situation.

There is so much fulfillment to be found in this world that we don't have to go struggling and striving for it. You have been blessed with more talent than you can ever use up. Why then give your life to striving to fulfill yourself in other areas? Why consider yourself a failure because you have been trying to inflict your will on a given set of circumstances, when you are an unbounded success when you use your own God-given talents. You can be a great success in this life, and all you have to do is to recognize those talents which are yours and yours alone and follow them wherever they may lead you.

Don't let your self-inflicted failures hold you back. Simply say: Well, that is not for me, I will release it and move on. Release it and move on and you will find the success that is justly yours.

Idea Number 32

• • •

A HOVEL OR A PALACE

What sort of environment, what sort of surroundings will you be spending your day in today? Will they be happy and bright surroundings, or will they be dull and rather miserable ones?

Charles Kingsley once was visited by a friend of his who had lived in the Himalayas. He came to Kingsley's tiny little cottage in a tiny little village and felt very, very sad for poor old Charles Kingsley and told him so and said, "How sad it must be to live in this little cottage in this tiny little out-of-the-way place while so much is going on around you out there in the wide, wide world; tiger hunts and all sorts of wonderful things." Kingsley turned to him with rather a happy, quiet smile and said, "You know, my friend, it is some years since I first realized that my dwelling place must be my prison or my palace. Thank God I made the right decision and that God has made my place a palace."

Think about this as you prepare for your day. Are you going to be working around the same house that you work around every day? Are you going to the same office or the same shop that you go to every day? Take another look at it. Open your eyes. Realize that of itself it has no existence. You and you alone have the power to make it what it is.

Have you begun to think of your home as ordinary? Rethink it today. Think it into a palace. Rejoice and polish and shine it and see it as your palace. Your office? Has it become a dull routine and a dowdy office for you? Take another look. See it as the palace in which you live your life and let it be worthy of the golden life that you are. Your life is yours to make and the environment in which you conduct that life is yours to make. You and you alone decide the nature of that environment. You have probably heard me say before that this is expressed most simply for me in the tiny little rhyme that says:

"Two men looked out from prison bars,
One saw mud but the other saw stars."

What are you going to see in your home, in your office, in your classroom, in your shop this day? Why not make it a palace, because only you have the power to make it a hovel or to make it a palace. Use the power of your creative imagination. Use the power of your own mind constructively and you shall live this day in a palace fit for a king or a queen.

Idea Number 33

• • •

PATIENCE

When I was young I was taught that patience is a virtue and, frankly, I found it quite annoying. It seemed to me that what it really meant was that you had to wait for what you wanted until some adult determined the right time for you to have it. But as I grew up a little, I began to realize that there is a great value to patience, particularly when you weigh it against the opposite; impatience. Oh, the cost of impatience; I guess patience is a virtue because impatience is costly. Think about the person who comes up and says I bought a new such-and-such car. You know very well that he hasn't done any such thing. What he has done is to put down a small sum of money to buy a car which he is going to pay on until perhaps the thing is worn out and he is still paying long after he has ceased enjoying the benefits of the purchase. That's a pretty high price to pay for impatience.

A while back I was talking to a friend of mine, a widowed lady, who isn't affluent by any means. She had just signed as guarantor for her son who was buying an electric guitar and she was terrified lest something went wrong with his purchase, and I asked, "Well, why did you do it?" She replied, "He just wouldn't wait." What a price to pay; while the young man is strumming away on his electric guitar, his widowed mother is dying a thousand deaths at the fear and cost of his impatience. The most tragic example I have come across recently is an article published in a local newspaper about a boy who had been sent away to a house of correction for stealing. He was asked by the judge if he asked his mother for the money, and wouldn't she have given it to him. He agreed that she would have done so. Which then led the judge to inquire why then did he steal the money? He said, "Well, sir, mom doesn't get home until 6:30 and the film began at 6:00. For thirty minutes this boy blotted his life. It really is tragic, the cost of impatience.

Sometimes the most expensive part of patience is in dealing with other people. That's not always easy. When some people aren't well, they become annoying and irritating and those who are nearest to them have to exercise their patience to the fullest. Bitter things are said and we have to admit that that is not really like the person, it is the illness speaking at the moment and not the wonderful person that you know. There is a cost, you see, to impatience whereas patience leaves us completely free. (Jesus Christ's patience was profound. Even at the trial he didn't flare up although he was unfairly accused. When they crucified Him, he said, "Father, forgive them for they know not what they do.") That's more than you and I can hope to achieve. But at least we can try in some measure to achieve that sort of patience and forebearance.

Just a word to young people—when you feel impatient with your mother and father, just as I used to be, when you do feel impatient with your folks because they want to know where you have been or what you're doing, it's not because they are being square; it's because they care. They do care tremendously and there is a great price to their care. Remember—the cost of impatience is vast and you never have to pay it if you just stop and think of the alternative.

Idea Number 34

• • •

NO SLAP-DASH LIFE

Are you looking forward to the jobs that you have to do and the tasks that have to be accomplished by you? Or, are you going to get through them as well as you can, just to get them done?

I was thinking about this as I walked along the street one day. I saw a man on a ladder painting and this man flopped his brush backwards and forwards, slap-dash, slap-dash. It seemed as if every stroke was an endeavor. He wasn't watching what he was doing, his eyes were somewhere else, he was simply slapping away with his brush and I thought, "oh my, what a terribly dull and boring existence."

Then a few minutes later, I walked into an office where a lady sat banging away on an old addressing machine, the one you crank and bang up and down. She was singing quietly to the banging of the machine and the machine was acting rather like a metronome, beating time to her song. I realized that it wasn't the metronome that was setting the pace of the work, it was the pace in her heart that was setting the pace of the machine and I immediately went back in my mind to a few seconds ago when I watched the slap-dash painter and, I thought, gee, I wish that man could come in here and see this woman doing this, with just the same sort of ordinary, tedious task. She was getting some real joy out of it.

It seems to me that we only get out of a task what we put into it and if we're going to do anything at all we ought to do it with zest, particularly if we are going to try to do something good or helpful. If we are going to do a good or helpful deed, we ought to do it with enthusiasm and zest.

If it is done merely as a duty, those people that we're seeking to benefit must feel the blight of our hard-heartedness. I thought of that painter, probably working lovingly to feed a wife and children, but I'm sure that the slap-dash nature of his endeavors had to interpenetrate their whole lives.

If any one of us is going to do anything to help anybody, we have to do it with ourself, to put some zeal, and some zest, a little bit of ourselves into it.

There are many people, particularly in churches, who spend a lot of their time and money on organized benevolence; on giving money or paying and thereby more or less absolving ourself from spontaneous acts of love and goodness.

Whatever you are going to do, do it zealously, thoroughly and lovingly even if you are polishing the silver. Polish your silver until it's fit for kings. Do your daily work, willingly, gratefully and happily.

When you give a gift, give yourself with zeal, give it with love. When you pray, don't just mumble prayers that have long lost their meaning. Pray with zeal. Your prayer should be vital and dynamic. It should be a piece of you.

We'll never get out of this rut of futility until we get back to a faith in something beyond ourselves. It seems to me that the sense of helplessness that hangs around over this old world of ours today, is like a fog that comes from a sense of our feebleness, comes from a slap-dash approach to life and to the world.

Whether your life is going to be a slap-dash life or whether it's going to tick and sing to the metronome of an inner joy, depends on you. Because you see the slap-dash or the joy is within you and you determine which will outpicture in your life and affairs.

Idea Number 35

• • •

THE NARROW MARGIN
OF FAILURE

I'm sure that you have seen a micrometer at one time or another. It's a very high-sounding name for a very simple little instrument. The micrometer is a little screw gauge which allows you to measure up to very fine limits, in fact, you can measure to one-thousandths of an inch in accuracy. When I first saw a micrometer I wondered why on earth anyone would want to measure to such fine limits and then I read about a building that collapsed killing a large number of people and costing hundreds of thousands of dollars in damage. An inquiry into the accident revealed that it was due to a miscalculation in thousandths of an inch.

Apparently the building had been assembled with iron girders without making sufficient allowance for the expansion and contraction of the beams. Due to changes in the temperature and a difference of thousandths of an inch, it caused a girder to snap and the building to fall and a large number of people to be killed.

Such a *narrow* margin, such a *tiny* margin between the stability of a strong building and the failure of a tumbling building, and I thought to myself—how similar this is to our own lives. There is such a *small* margin sometimes between success and failure. We all know individuals and organizations who have worked for years struggling in developing or building toward an objective and then just when the objective appeared to be in sight, they ran out of faith, hope and strength and abandoned their project right when they were on the verge of success.

Henry Austin wrote a beautiful little verse that sums this up admirably. He says:

"Twixt failure and success the point's so fine
That men sometimes know not
When they've touched the line.
Just when the pearl was waiting one more
    plunge,
How many divers have simply given up the
    sponge?
For there is honey even in the bitterest cup
And there is no failure save in giving up."

"There is no failure save in giving up." There is such a tiny margin between success and failure, and it is only *your* determination which can bridge that *tiny* margin of a few thousandths of an inch—one more try that will lead from seeming *failure* to abundant *success*, and so many people give up just when success was theirs for the asking.

Yes, my friend, the micrometer measures down to thousandths of an inch and you may be at this moment, thousandths of an inch, micro-seconds of time from your greatest success. One more effort is all it takes. There is no failure save in giving up.

Idea Number 36

• • •

LIFE BY THE INCH

One of my favorite fruits is the pomegranate. We used to call them "Indian Apples." I don't know how they got that name, but when I was a little boy, one of my greatest pleasures was to take a nickel along to the grocer's shop and buy a pomegranate.

They are a beautiful fruit, but there is one very interesting thing about a pomegranate. Although the seeds inside are beautifully sweet and juicy, they are separated into small compartments by a thin yellow skin that is very bitter and, therefore, if you try to bite into a pomegranate you get a mouthful of rather bitter material that is very unpleasant.

If, however, you eat your pomegranate one seed at a time, it is indeed a delicacy. This is exactly how it is with your life. You cannot live your life as a large lump—you can only live your life one day at a time. If you cut yourself, you don't heal in a moment. Your healing begins the very moment that you cut yourself and it progresses day by day, minute by minute. You don't get an education in one lump—it is one day's schooling followed by the next day's schooling.

You don't recover from the loss of a dear one overnight. Your bereavement is a process and it is only as you learn to live your life anew, day by day, that you overcome the loss and begin to build a new life.

The simple truth then is that you cannot live life by the *lump*. You have to live life *day by day* and this means patience and industry in building the type of life that you want. If you have a stiff limb, this day, try to bend it a little more. If you have been ill, this day, try to feel just a little better. Try to recognize yourself as recovered just a little and these little by little, day by day movements lead to the fulfillment and completion of the things you want in your life.

If you face a massive problem today, don't try to bite it off in one chunk. Try to make today's solution today and you are that much further forward towards the solution of the whole problem. If you look ahead at all your problems, then life can look pretty big. If you have children to educate, elderly loved ones to tend and care for, and a multitude of responsibilities, life can indeed look like quite a formidable trial.

But you don't *have* to deal with the problems of life, do you? You only *have* to deal with the problems of this one day. If there is, therefore, one simple thought I can leave you that will help you to do this, it is just this one simple thought: "Life by the mile can be a trial, but life by the inch is a cinch!" You don't have to solve the problems of life, you only have to meet the problems of this day. You only have to endure the pain of this moment. "Life by the mile is a trial, but life by the inch is a cinch!"

Idea Number 37

• • •

THE LOBSTER POT

Do you enjoy lobsters? Most people in New England, where I'm from, do. Has it ever occurred to you how they get their lobsters? I am sure you have seen a lobster pot. It is a very simple device that allows a lobster to make an easy entry into the pot, but provides a very difficult egress. There are many, many things in our lives like this.

We human beings tend to enter all too often into situations, circumstances or commitments without really considering how we will get out of them and what sort of obligation they are going to entail. So many of us are ready to sign on the dotted line without giving too much thought to just exactly what we are undertaking.

I am sure that a great deal of family unhappiness and human suffering comes from the refusal to think of the obligations when we are about to sign for the benefits. You know the sort of thing I mean. This applies to all sorts of aspects of our lives, to borrowing, to signing notes or contracts of all sorts, to joining things. Many people are great joiners. They enter into things like mortgages, even marriages, too easily.

It is so easy to sign, so easy to accept, so easy to say YES, so easy to make commitments and then perhaps so hard to fulfill, so long to pay back, so long to grieve and regret, so long to repent. Obligations are so easy to get into and sometimes so hard to fulfill and all too often we find the joys that we have been seeking in taking these obligations are nothing but mirages. We follow the crowd, we follow fashion, we cling to our personal pride, we make commitments and shortsighted decisions just to try to keep up with other people. Should we not look beyond the moment and beyond the immediate pleasure to all the costs and all the implications, to all the days that are to come, and to the debt that is due and the payment that will be required. The obligation, the attendance, the time, whatever it may be that we have to pay to meet our commitment should not be lightly undertaken. Commitments we make carry with them obligations beyond the limits of time.

We should keep ourselves as clear as we can of questionable commitments; take a long look at life and consider all commitments carefully in the clear light of reason and proceed slowly before signing on the dotted line and acting like the lobster.

Commitments are easy to enter, they may not be easy to fulfill and sometimes they are almost impossible to get out of.

Idea Number 38

• • •

PAIN OR PRECEPT

Once when the great Gautama Buddha was teaching the people of a small village, he reached into his garment and withdrew a little brown pebble and said, "Behold that which is my teacher!" He then explained how he had been walking along the trail that day and had failed to notice the beauty on all sides of him until the little pebble had fallen into his sandal. He was forced to pause to remove it and in so doing, suddenly became aware of the blue of the sky, the beauty of the trees, the fragrance of the flowers along the trail, even the vivid colors of a butterfly. He said, "I was walking through so much beauty and yet failed to notice it until this little pebble caused me to pause. Surely, is not this the folly of man, that he is taught more readily by pain than by precept?"

It is unfortunately *true* that often we *are* taught more readily by pain than by precept. There are always two roads open to us as we journey through life—the road of compulsion and the road of election. We can choose consciously to cooperate with Creative Intelligence. We can choose to grow, to improve ourself, to change for the better. But, if we don't *choose* to do so, we will be *forced* to do so. The law will wield a progressive hand. If we are not growing through choice, we will be forced to grow through the lessons of experience, and experience can be a very harsh teacher as some of us already know.

A lot of people think that a war is being raged between the forces of good and evil. There is no evidence of *two* powers clashing in the universal creative plan. Then, what is the cause of humanity's suffering and problems? It is man's imperfect understanding. As man's understanding is lifted up, so will his world be lifted out of chaos and destruction.

Behind every success, or every seeming miracle of healing, there is a very simple cause—an *idea*. An idea can make a million dollars; it can heal an incurable disease. It can rebuild an entire life! If you are open to new ideas, new ideas will *come* to you. Sometimes they come as direct illumination; sometimes they take a more circuitous route and seek you out from the pages of a book, the conversation of a friend, or the voice of a teacher. *Ideas* are the way out of those self-imposed limitations which can be a prison and a hell. All you need in order to bring about the healing of any situation in your life is a new *idea*. That is why meditation is such an important part of successful living—it opens you to inspiration and understanding. When you meditate on a regular basis, you will never fail to receive ideas. Perhaps, not always *during* meditation, but they will come.

There is one idea, active in mind, that can resurrect the life of anyone. It can move you steadily upward to ever-higher levels of prosperity, power and success. This is the idea or the realization that *all things work together for good. LIVE* by this idea, this faith, and you will be able to overcome all of life's challenges. You will discover that you *are* a better, a greater person because of your experiences in life. Every experience will be transmuted into strength of character.

Idea Number 39

• • •

YESTERDAY'S ACHIEVEMENTS

Do you sometimes think there's not enough reward for some of the things that you've done in this life? Do you sometimes look out and say, "Well, you know things shouldn't be like this, things shouldn't be this way, because after all, remember I did this or I did thus some time ago"? Are you a person that tries to live off yesterday's attainments? It's a fateful way to go through life, believe me. Nobody wants to eat yesterday's cold potatoes and nobody can live on yesterday's achievements. How many times do you find somebody that had done one major thing in their life, that first writes a major book about it, then writes a minor book about it, then writes a pamphlet about it, and then distorts their whole life trying to get people to remember one thing that they did. When we try to live on yesterday's glories, we die today. Think about it!

A number of military officers once approached Napoleon to recommend a young captain for a very special promotion; so Napoleon asked, "Why do you propose this particular fellow?'' They answered that through unusual courage and cleverness and daring, he'd won a very significant victory several days before. Napoleon thought about it for a moment and said, ''Good, but what did he do the next day?'' Nobody knows what they replied, but that was the last that was ever heard of that young man. You see, there are two kinds of people in this world of ours; there are those who show an occasional outburst of brilliance, and there are those who can be depended upon day after day to do their best every single day of the year. In other words, there are the flushers, the flashers and the plodders. Believe me, that once you get into your mind this idea, that by one single flash of brilliance you can earn enough days, you live in ashes. Today's reward is for today's endeavor; today's love brings back today's love. You can't say, ''Oh, how I loved her yesterday, why does she not love me today?'' If you want to be loved today, you must love today, tomorrow's love is not yet here, yesterday's love is spent and returned. TODAY'S REWARDS COME FROM TODAY'S EFFORTS. You cannot borrow on yesterday's glory and still live a meaningful life. Be glad for the achievements of yesterday, yes, but don't feed your consciousness, your pride, your self-image upon them; that's like feeding them cold potatoes. Make one minor achievement today and live on that. If you can make another major achievement, fine, but if you can't, feed yourself on the achievements of today.

Love, laugh, share, help, live today, and accept the rewards of life for today's effort, and then you'll be living on today's Spiritual food, and not on the cold potatoes of yesterday's attainments.

Idea Number 40

• • •

WATCH YOUR WORDS

How careful are you in choosing your words? Let's stop for a few moments and think about the importance of every single word we speak.

You see, a word is more than a mere sign or symbol. It is a magnet! It is filled with the idea it represents. It is alive with the power of the idea it expresses. Therefore, the continued use of any word that connotes error, negation, or destructiveness, keeps error, negation and destructiveness alive in your mind. By our words we often feed and keep alive the very condition we want to overcome. Remember that you have to think it before you can say it—and the thoughts that fill your mind will fill your life with their image.

You know, nearly everyone talks too much! You can avoid a lot of unhappiness in your world if you will test the fitness of your words by making them pass through three narrow gates. First, is it needed? Second, is it true, and finally, is it kind? If you were to follow this simple method, many words will be left unspoken. Are they necessary? Are they true? Are they kind?

Speak only constructively to those around you. Speak with understanding and sincerity. Be honest. You can't try to boost a friend's morale with good words and at the same time be silently thinking, "you deserve just what you are getting."

We don't realize how far our spoken word travels or whom it reaches. To watch your words constantly may be difficult in the beginning, but with persistence you can form the right habit of thinking and speaking. You may find a bit of help through the simple process of cancellation. Remember when you studied arithmetic? You found cancellation a quick and easy method of solving a lot of problems. You can use this same cancellation when destructive words are spoken. Cancel unkind remarks with kind ones. Everytime you catch yourself thinking a destructive thought, immediately cancel it with a constructive one. Do this over and over, a thousand times a day if necessary. In the evening it is a good feeling to be able to say, "Today I lived, thought and spoke as much good as I could."

Your words do have power. Your word is, after all, only the garment of your thought—and the quality of your thought determines what comes into your experience. The reason for this is that the subconscious mind is a passive servant. It accepts good or evil suggestions—your subconscious mind does not care which. It works all suggestions out to their logical conclusions in your human affairs. In creative activity the first logical step is thought. The next is the spoken word. We are thinking constantly. When thoughts are put into words, their creative power in our lives becomes intensified. Therefore, we have thoughts, words, and conditions in a logical sequence. Remember: thought, word and then the condition in your life! That's the inevitable sequence!

Material things are always in a state of flux because the law of matter is change. When we speak sincere words of Truth, positive words, constructive words, we are speaking the kind of words that will create ideal conditions. The only reason why ideal conditions are not more universally manifested is that we speak so many mutable words. Like a seesaw, our words are first up and then down—first constructive then destructive. Resolve now to watch your spoken words—they are important to you and your life.

Idea Number 41

• • •

NOT SO EASY

Most of us have taken some sort of aptitude test at one time or other. In this day and age it seems almost everything that a young person is going to do, or anyone going to be employed, is apt to have themselves measured quite considerably by the tests that they have to take.

Awhile back I read some interesting remarks made by a leader in the field of human engineering, a Dr. Johnson O'Connor of the Stevens Institute. Now O'Connor was asked once if there was ever a person who did poorly in all the battery of tests. There are so many different tests that it would seem unlikely that there would be any human being who didn't do well in one of them. But O'Connor laughed and said, "Oh, yes, there is a type of person who does badly in all the tests we offer. About one person in 8,000 is absolutely hopeless in all of the tests." So he was asked, "What do you do about such a person?" O'Connor said, "Do? We don't worry about him. He never presents us with a problem.

He is usually the president of his firm or is self-employed.''

Well, this didn't make any sense to the interviewer. So he went on to question O'Connor about this. "How can it be that a man whose tests show that he has little native ability is able to go on and become the president of a corporation?" O'Connor explained it very simply. He said, "Since nothing ever came easy to such a person, he learned in his youth to work hard and long. The working hard and long provides him with much great inner strength, courage and experience which is real knowledge, and it is this which makes him a success."

I thought about this. I thought to myself, "Goodness, shouldn't we learn from this in our own life?" When the winds of difficulty blow around us; when we begin to feel inadequate to cope with a situation; we should learn that the winds of difficulty blow around us in order that we might get a bit stronger. Think what would happen if you planted a sapling in a greenhouse and waited until it was full grown to plant it out on a mountain top. It wouldn't last one winter, would it? It is the sapling that grows strong in the early winters of its life that becomes the strong tree that can live and survive in its native world.

It is the same with human beings. It is in the meeting and overcoming of our own problems that we grow, and isn't this terribly important in regard to our own children? If we protect them from the growing experience; if we make it easy, too easy for them all the way, they don't have the opportunity to learn this secret that Dr. O'Connor talks about: the secret of having to work hard and long, of having to learn, of having to gain experience instead of having it fed to them on a plate.

It is the life which is exposed to problems, it is the person to whom everything doesn't come easy that growth comes in firm strength. It is the tree that is exposed to the March winds that can stand the hurricane. It is the life that is allowed to experience and overcome difficulties that becomes the fulfilled life.

Idea Number 42

• • •

EARTHWORMS FOR
FEATHERS

Are you aware of the importance of every single
choice you make? Are you aware how far any tiny
decision that you make may take you? It's an interesting thought, you know, that every decision that
we make colors our attitudes, and our attitudes color
the next decision we make and so it's sort of a
spiral. If you make negative decisions, they induce a
negative frame of mind, and that makes it easier to
make negative decisions. If you make a positive
decision, that engenders a positive state of mind, and
it's easier to make positive decisions.

Every choice has a natural result leading to further
choices of a similar nature. Luther Burbank, the
plant wizard, once told a marvelous fable about a
young skylark that impresses the importance of the
choices we make. This young skylark was out flying
one day with his father and heard his father tell
stories about what fine birds skylarks are. He heard
that they can fly higher and sing more sweetly than
any other bird and the father went on impressing

upon his son the fact that to be a skylark was to come from a very fine family, to have a worthy lineage and to live a lofty and beautiful life. But all the time he was listening, the little skylark had one ear to the ground, because he could see far below a man walking along a roadway pushing a handcart and on this handcart was a tiny silver bell that was tinkling very clearly, and so overcome with curiosity, the little skylark suddenly dived towards the earth like a plummet, just as skylarks always have done; they soar upwards in graceful, sweeping spirals, singing as they mount, and then they descend. They drop straight downward, and that's a lot like man who can climb upward only with great effort, but can plunge down very rapidly from step to step.

And so it was the little skylark flying around with his papa, hearing about his wondrous lineage—he heard also the tinkling bell on the handcart and dived down towards the ground, and he heard the man saying, "Earthworms for trade for skylark feathers, earthworms for trade for skylark feathers!" It seemed a strange thing the little man was shouting, but the little skylark thought earthworms a great delicacy and so he asked, "How many worms do you give for a feather?" The man replied, "Two worms for a single feather." So the skylark plucked a feather from his tail, made a trade and ate his two worms with great relish. Then he spiralled upward again to join his father, hoping that his father wouldn't notice the absence of a feather from his plumage and father skylark didn't notice. But day after day the young bird did the same thing, exchanging feathers for earthworms, until one morning, he discovered, when he lifted his wings, he couldn't fly. So many of his feathers were missing that his wings could no longer bear his weight up into the air. So, for long months, while his feathers were growing out again, the little skylark had ample time to repent his foolish bargain of earthworms for skylark feathers and to regret the choice he had made. So it is with us, as we make our daily choices. We either trade good experience for even better ones, or we trade earthworms for skylark feathers. Every decision you make leads you onward and upward or downward and downward, every single choice.

Idea Number 43

• • •

YOU ARE NOT ALONE

Sometimes I think that we feel completely help-less in the job of remaking this world of ours. Do you feel impotent to make your life, your home, your town, your family and your world any better? Well, if you do, let me tell you of a simple incident that changed my mind on this subject.

One time I visited a bee farm where beehives are kept and maintained. It was in the middle of the summer, and as I walked from hive to hive there was a strange swishing noise rather like the sound of the sea coming up from the shore. I asked the old bee-keeper what it was about and he explained to me that these were Fanner Bees. Yes, Fanner Bees. Inside the hive were thousands of bees that stood there with their heads down turned towards the center of the hive and their wings were beating as rapidly as they could. What they actually did was to draw the bad air out through one side of the entrance and draw clean air in from the other side so that the whole hive was air-conditioned by these thousands of Fanner Bees. They did nothing but fan air through the hive to keep the honey beautiful and sweet smelling. I thought to myself, I wonder what the individual Fanner Bee must think? There he is fanning his wings; he isn't making any impression—one tiny bee—what can one tiny bee do? But you see, when his effort is added to the other thousands of Fanner Bees, there we find a perfect air-conditioning system for the hive. I continued to think to myself, "Isn't this just like our human life? Of myself, I can do nothing, but where two or more are gathered together, ah, there's a difference."

You are probably thinking at this moment, "Yes, wouldn't it be good if a group of people got together to air-condition this troubled world of ours, to fan out guilt, hatred, misery, fear and doubt, but here I am, all alone, what can I do?" You are not alone. Many people feel as you do. By joining our total consciousness, we are a tremendous force, just like that whole force of Fanner Bees.

So, don't think how helpless you are, just think of how many people feel as you do and resolve right now that we are going to be the Fanner Bees of this day. We're going to air-condition this world of ours by fanning out fear, doubt, dislike, discouragement and all negative thoughts. Instead, we are going to start fanning into our world love, light, laughter, joy and inquisitive wonder.

Everyone of us can add the flap of our wings to the wings of angels glorifying this world and all together we are a mighty force for air-conditioning this world for good.

Idea Number 44

• • •

LISTEN FOR THE MEANING

Did you ever hear the story about the human ear that caused a war?

It's true, you know. There was a time when one human ear caused a great international war. The ear belonged to an English sea captain whose name was Jenkins and the Spaniards thought that Captain Jenkins wasn't as honest as he might be. In fact, they were quite convinced that he was a pirate, so they captured Captain Jenkins and simply cut off his ear. Jenkins, righteously indignant, brought the rest of himself and his ear back to England and complained to the Monarch about this terrible rough handling. At that time, the English were just spoiling for a war with the Spaniards and they were able to use this incident to launch the great war called, "THE WAR OF JENKINS' EAR." If you don't believe me, go look it up, it's absolutely true. There was once a war between England and Spain known as "THE WAR OF JENKINS' EAR." Now, what I want to ask you is, will there be a war of your ear this day? I wonder how many days your ears draw you into war? You see the educated ear is a selective instrument. It doesn't just hear the vibrations of somebody's larnyx, it hears the feelings, the sufferings, the anguish, the difficulty, the joy, the love and whatever lies behind the words. The educated ear avoids so many wars which might otherwise have been caused.

Now, as you go out into your world today, ask yourself—"How educated is my ear?" If somebody comes up to you and in the middle of a conversation they say to you, "WHY DON'T YOU MIND YOUR OWN BUSINESS?" what do you hear? Do you hear anger, hurt, hatred, resentment? Or do you hear somebody who is saying, "I AM HURT ON THE INSIDE. I DON'T KNOW HOW TO DEAL WITH THIS PROBLEM? I DON'T WANT TO TALK ABOUT IT POSSIBLY BECAUSE I'M ASHAMED. HELP ME SOMEHOW TO OVERCOME THIS PROBLEM INSIDE ME." Is that what you hear or do you hear, "Mind your own business," as a declaration of war? Do you then stomp off to your desk or stomp off to your own kitchen? War is declared, unspoken war and silence reigns between good friends for a long time. Or what about when you're out today and somebody says to you, "WHY DON'T YOU GET OUT OF MY WAY?" Do you feel rejection? Do you feel hatred or are you able to sense in somebody else a deep sense of inner frustration or loneliness? Do you listen behind the words, "Get out of my way," and see a hurt, bruised soul? Is your ear educated enough not to go to war over the phrase "Get out of my way?"

You see, if you are going to serve your Creator and your fellowman in the truest sense, you will walk through your world with an educated ear. When you do this, you will bring peace and harmony to the world about you and you will never have a "War of Jenkins' Ear."

Idea Number 45

• • •

THE LIMITED VIEW

Does it seem to you that at times your life is hopelessly tangled, the threads of your life become totally enmeshed and you can't see your way out and life becomes so complicated that you wonder if it's even worth going on?

Well, when we become perplexed by difficulties and seeming inconsistencies of life, we should remember that at any one moment we have only a partial view of things and that a partial view of anything never shows the thing as it really is. We simply get *one* viewpoint. Any time that we see a particular segment as a whole, we see it in a limited fashion. We can't hope to understand the whole pattern from our limited view.

For example, supposing you were to show an Eskimo any number of pictures of parts of a camel; the Eskimo had never seen a camel; you might show his rear legs and a hump and a long neck and a head; he could never get an *overall* view of what a camel really looked like.

The other illustration that I like to think of in terms of confused lives and perplexity is the comparison with a Persian rug. It is said that if you saw only the *under* side of a Persian rug, it would seem to be an absolute jumble of lines and colors with no beauty and no apparent pattern or logic. But this would be only because we didn't have the key—we couldn't see the whole. If you then turned the rug over, you'd see it from the *right* side and you would recognize the pattern, you would realize that the chaotic threads underneath were making up a beautiful and consistent whole.

Now this is exactly the way it is with your life, and someday when we have all had enough of spiritual growth in this human classroom, we will come to see that the various threads that have gone to make up this human life, the seeming disjointed happenings, the jumble of events, the apparent accidents, were really a part of an orderly, beautiful and perfect pattern—the wrap of something splendid, that we are steadily weaving with and for our Creator.

If your life seems like a meaningless jumble of events, it simply means that from where you stand at this moment, your viewpoint enables you to see only a tiny segment of the whole. If we can stand back a little further, we see more of the whole, but even then, we have to wait until we achieve a high degree of Spiritual unfoldment, to recognize that within this jumble of events is woven the pattern of Perfection.

The Creator doesn't make mistakes. Know that whatever is happening in your life right now is part of a pattern of Perfection.

Idea Number 46

• • •

DON'T BREAK THE KEY

Did you ever break a key in a lock? I was looking at a bunch of keys on a friend's key ring and I discovered that there was one that only had the shank on it. The key was completely broken off. I said to him, "How did that happen?" He said, "Well, I had the key in the door and just kept turning." Now I think that's like most of us at times. We want things to work out our way even though we have the wrong key in the lock. We want the key to turn. We insist that it comes out our way and all we succeed in doing is to break the key. You know, there was a right key for that lock that my friend was trying to open, and had he chosen the right key, it would have turned very, very easily. Most of us are like this. We want to turn the keys the way we want them in our human relationships.

Have you ever noticed how perturbed we get when other people tend to do something differently from the way that we would have done it or when other people seem to make wrong decisions, they decide differently from the way we would have decided? We become very angry when somebody else drops the ball, misses an opportunity or fails to grab onto something that we think we would have grabbed onto. We are all inclined to do our share of side-line coaching and trying to force our key into the locks of other people's lives. It isn't easy, is it, to sit by and watch somebody else do something in a manner which you think is less efficient than the way you could do it. This is never more true than when we're dealing with children. Children don't do things as well as we do; their fingers aren't nimble as ours are and it's such a great temptation to grab something out of their hands and do it for them. We try to force the key of our understanding in the lock of their young minds, and this is not the way to help them grow.

Life has to be learned by everyone. If only the skillful and capable people were permitted to do things, there would be no chance for anyone else to learn those skills and capabilities. Almost anyone can learn to make their own way; and the most successful leaders are those who discover early in their lives that there's no good reason or purpose to be served in putting square pegs into round holes, or in trying to force the wrong keys into the right keyholes. We have to take people as we find them and then help them to be useful in their own way, not in ours. We'll never find anyone who will do anything the way we would do it. Once we recognize that, then we stop chafing at the bit, we stop trying to force the key of our life into the lock of other people's existence and we allow them to grow in their own way. I think it's summed up beautifully for me in a little poem that says:

"And in self-judgment, if you find your deeds to others are superior, To you Providence has been kind, and you should be so to those inferior."

Examples shed a genial ray of light which men are apt to borrow, so *first improve yourself today and then improve your friends tomorrow.*

Do that, and you'll be a better self and they'll be better friends or children.

Idea Number 47

• • •

SELF-DISCIPLINE

In the Wadi Natrun in the Thevayid Desert in Egypt, right in the middle of a desert, miles and miles from any water or from any living thing, there grows an almond tree. Yes, an almond tree, right in the blankest, bleakest desert you can imagine and it gets there as a result of self-discipline.

In the year 346, there was an old monk named Abba Amoy and he was in the desert praying with one of his pupils and Abba Amoy was trying to teach the pupil about the fruits of self-discipline and the pupil found it difficult to understand the principles that the old monk was teaching him. So the monk took his stick, which was an almond branch, and stuck it on the sand. Then he said to his pupil, whose name was John, the Short:

"Water this," he told John, the Short, "until it bears fruit and you will know what I mean." Well, the spot was miles and miles from the nearest well, but that night, when it got cool, John, the Short, walked all the way to the well, filled his jar with water, and walked back and watered the stick. He did this every single night for three years and at the end of three years, the stick began to bear fruit. When it did, John, the Short, took the kernels to the nearby monastery and said to the monks, "Behold, the fruits of self-discipline."

Are you at the moment living in a mental desert? Are you faced with sickness, loneliness, family problems, business problems, money worries, that make it feel as though you are living in the middle of a desert? Then let me tell you: That desert can flourish, just as the almond tree did, into everything you need, with self-discipline. By this I mean the discipline of your own mind.

Do as old John, the Short, did and *constantly* become aware of that which you are thinking and discipline your thoughts so as only to think of the good. Also, refuse to allow defeat or negative thoughts to enter your mind. Water your mind with thoughts of love, health, joy, peace and harmony and you will have the fruits of self-discipline blossom and flourish in the desert of your present experience, no matter what it may be.

Idea Number 48

• • •

"UP" THE "DOWN" STAIRCASE

If you are like most people in America, you will hustle and bustle through every single moment of the day. I wonder just how much of this hustling and bustling is really necessary for maximum production.

I remember when I was a young boy, my parents would take me to a department store that had an escalator. I would always run ahead of them to the escalator, to the moving staircase, and start to run up the "down" staircase. I'm sure everyone has tried it. It's an interesting procedure. You run like mad and stay in the same place while other people on the staircase are not running at all and yet they're going somewhere and, you know, human life is so much like this.

Activity doesn't always mean action. Sometimes we do the most when we appear to be doing nothing. A lot of time is wasted in fussing over nonessentials. We can ill afford this extravagant output of wasted strength. Sooner or later we simply have to decide what is important and what is not important because if we try to do everything at once we'll end up by doing more harm than good.

The mind is a delicate and complex instrument subject to strains and stresses from within and without. Too much pressure can often result in a breakdown. Mental fatigue can be far more exhausting than bodily weariness. As I see it, there is only one way to keep going and that's by constant communication with the Source within us, the Source of all life and vitality.

There is a point of stillness at the hub of the whirling wheel of time and it's to that center that we must learn to withdraw if we are not to be broken on the spokes or fall off the edge. Quietness at the heart of activity is the only place where God can get to us, so if we want peace, we must put ourselves in a position to receive it. This is the secret of the renewal of mental, physical and spiritual strength.

Having found this place within you, you will experience the confidence of mind that has found its true center. A mind that has found its true center has found a place of poise like an ant walking along a balance beam who finds the center and the beam is stationary. So it is with us.

Among your hustling and bustling take time out to be still and say, "Am I really running up the 'down' staircase?" All too often we are with our own will running against the tide of life. If you find yourself running up the "down" staircase, swiftly get off and stand still on the "up" staircase, and that "up" staircase is a staircase of quiet meditation.

Idea Number 49

• • •

THE SIN OF OMISSION

Here is a beautiful poem by Margaret Sangster. It's called, "The Sin of Omission":

"It isn't the thing that you do, dear; it is the thing that you leave undone.

That gives you a bit of heartache. At the setting of the sun.

The tender word forgotten. The letter you didn't write,

The flowers you didn't send, dear. Are your haunting ghosts at night.

The stone that you might have lifted out of a brother's way.

A bit of kindly counsel. You were too hurried to say:

The loving touch of a hand, dear; the gentle winning tone;

But you had no time nor thought for, with troubles enough of your own.

Those little acts of kindness, so easily out of mind

Those chances to be an angel, which we poor
   mortals find;
They come in night and silence, each sad re-
   proachful wraith,
When hope is faint and flagging, and a chill
   falls on our faith;
For life is all too short, dear, and sorrow is all
   too great
To suffer our slow compassion, that tarries until
   it's too late.
And it isn't the thing you do, dear, it's the
   thing you leave undone,
That will give you a bit of a heartache, at the
   setting of the sun.''

What is it that lies before you to do this day, to
gladden somebody else's life, that in a short while,
when you no longer have the opportunity, will hang
heavy on your heart, if you haven't done it? Perhaps
it is the love you wanted to share with a parent, or a
child, or a loved one, or the patching up of a quarrel
that's gone on too long.

Life is too short, my friend. Spend this day catch-
ing up. Do it today. Express the love that remains
unexpressed; forgive the error that remains unforgiven
in your heart; patch up that quarrel that needs patching up. You have this day to repair all the ravages of
time and to do that which is right and that which is
loving. Why not reach out to someone today and
overcome the Sin of Omission. I guarantee it will
make your life so much happier.

Idea Number 50

• • •

VOICE OR ECHO?

Are you a voice or an echo? It seems to me that with the vast increases in human knowledge and with the magnificent inventions by which knowledge is disseminated and spread around, we're all in danger of just becoming plain parrots, the echo of someone else's opinions.

From our daily newspapers, from cinemas, from television, books and platforms come voices of other people telling us what we should think; telling us how to live or what to believe. I'm one of these. I sit here and try to share ideas with you, and as I was thinking about this, I thought, "There is a grave danger that you will allow my thinking to become your thinking." I suddenly realize that I'm not really trying to get you to think what I think. What I'm really trying to do is to get you to think for *yourself*. Take the ideas that I communicate, take them away and hassle them within yourself.